SWINDON TO NEWPORT

Vic Mitchell and Keith Smith

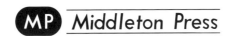
MP Middleton Press

Cover picture: Roaring up the gradient from the Severn Tunnel and entering Patchway is no. 3407 Madras, *a 4-4-0 of the "Bulldog" class. The scene is between the wars and includes goods loop signals on the left. (G.H.Soole/P.Q.Treloar coll.)*

I. Map to show the diversionary routes available between Swindon and Newport in 1948. The Severn Bridge was in use until 26th October 1960. (Railway Magazine)

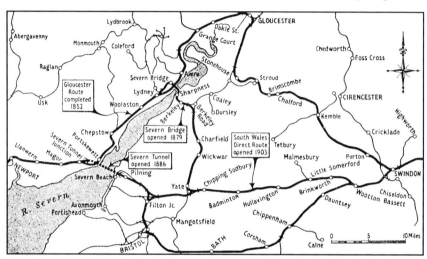

Published April 2004

ISBN 1 904474 30 6

© *Middleton Press, 2004*

Design   David Pede
Typesetting   Barbara Mitchell

Published by
          Middleton Press
          Easebourne Lane
          Midhurst, West Sussex
          GU29 9AZ
Tel: 01730 813169
Fax: 01730 812601
Email: info@middletonpress.co.uk
www.middletonpress.co.uk

Printed & bound by MPG Books Ltd, Bodmin, Cornwall

INDEX

ACKNOWLEDGEMENTS

We are grateful to many of those mentioned in the credits for their assistance and also to, W.R. Burton, R.Caston (Welsh Railways Research Circle), L.Crosier, G.Croughton, S.P. Derek, N.Langridge, National Motor Museum, K.Robertson, Mr D. & Dr. S.Salter and finally our ever helpful wives, Barbara Mitchell and Janet Smith.

II. Railway Clearing House map for 1947.

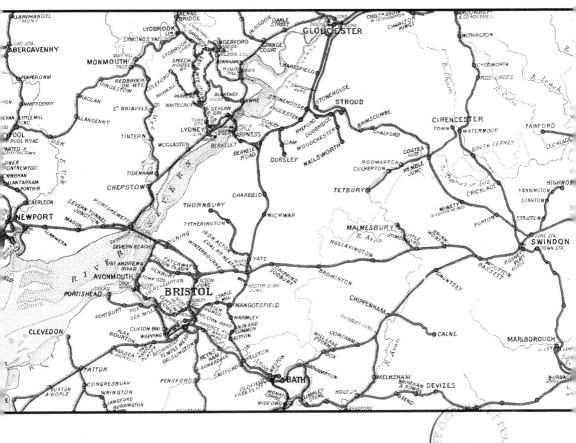

GEOGRAPHICAL SETTING

The old established market town of Swindon expanded greatly following the arrival of the railway and its associated works. The first 20 miles or so of the route are mostly on Clays, the track dipping to pass over the south flowing River Avon, west of Little Somerford.

A steady climb takes the route onto the Oolitic Limestone of the Cotswold Hills, through which it runs in Sodbury Tunnel. East of this, the line passes from Wiltshire into Gloucestershire and west of it there is a steady descent to the Severn Tunnel, over a distance of almost 20 miles.

Coal Measures are traversed for about four miles in the vicinity of Coalpit Heath and thereafter the route is mostly on Marl for the remainder of its length.

After passing through the Severn Tunnel in a variety of strata, the line emerges onto the coastal plain of what was and is Monmouthshire, it having been Gwent for an interval. Newport and its extensive docks developed mainly on the land at the confluence of the River Usk and the Ebbw River. Newport became a city in 2002, independent of Monmouthshire. This county is part of Wales again.

The maps are to the scale of 25 ins to 1 mile with north at the top, unless otherwise indicated.

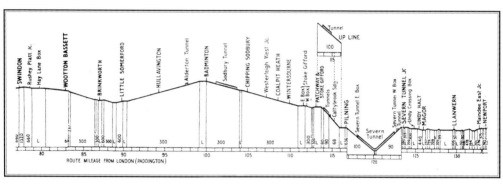

III. Gradient profile.

HISTORICAL BACKGROUND

Great Western Railway trains from London were passing the site of Swindon station to a temporary terminus three miles to the west of it at Hay Lane from 17th December 1840. They continued on to Bristol from 30th June 1841. However, a station was not provided at Swindon until July 1842, although the line northwards to Cirencester opened in May 1841.

Another early line in the area was that of the Bristol & Gloucester Railway which opened in 1844 and became part of the Midland Railway in 1845. The South Wales Railway opened on 18th June 1850 between Chepstow and Swansea, it becoming part of the GWR in 1862.

The final line to consider as an ultimate component of the subject of this volume was the single track Bristol & South Wales Union Railway of 1863, which ran from a ferry terminal on the shore of the Severn Estuary to Bristol, via Patchway.

All the above mentioned lines were laid to the broad gauge of 7ft 0¼ins, but were converted to standard gauge, the last two mentioned in 1872. Part of the B&SWUR became the eastern approach to the Severn Tunnel and was doubled in 1887. The tunnel came into use for passenger trains on 1st December 1886 (goods from 1st September 1886) after a protracted construction period. The Act had been passed on 27th June 1872 and work began in March 1873, but several floodings ensued.

Following the opening of the Severn Tunnel, all London services, including many slow moving coal trains, had to travel via Bristol. The eastern part of the route in this album was a late addition which helped the GWR to lose its alternative meaning of Great Way Round.

A shorter route between London and South Wales was required and thus an Act was obtained on 23rd July 1896 to construct double track between Wootton Bassett and Patchway. The first sod was cut on 29th November 1897 and the line was opened to passengers on 1st July 1903. The connections between it and the Malmesbury branch and also the Midland Railway are chronicled in the captions of the pictures of those locations. The numerous station closures are similarly described.

The route and the rest of the GWR came into the Western Region of British Railways upon nationalisation in 1948. Privatisation preparations in March 1994 resulted in InterCity operating between Swindon and South Wales, with Regional Railways running trains from the South Coast to South Wales. The former became part of the franchise of Great Western Trains on 4th February 1996 and the latter was operated by Prism Rail's Wales & West from October 13th of that year. This company also provided services between Newport and Gloucester, while Virgin CrossCountry ran some trains between Bristol and Newport. Some operational names have changed subsequently.

PASSENGER SERVICES

Down trains are considered in this section. Initially there was only a local service through the Severn Tunnel, it operating between Bristol and Cardiff, with ten trains on weekdays and three on Sundays. From July 1887, a through train between London and New Milford was added, but the journey time between Swindon and Cardiff was the same as that via Gloucester.

The Midland Railway received serious competition for the Bristol - Manchester traffic on 2nd July 1888, when a joint GWR/LNWR service began via the Maindee East Curve. This avoided reversing at Newport. There were three trains each weekday, two of which were extended to Edinburgh. The frequency rose progressively to seven by 1908, having been extended westward in 1892, eventually to Penzance.

An express between London and Cardiff via Bristol began operating in 1891 and there were two from 1896. The opening of the line via Badminton brought some direct trains, notably the "South Wales Corridor Express" which left Paddington at 3.5pm and ran non-stop to Cardiff. It arrived at 6.30, having slipped a coach at Badminton. There was a repeat performance at 6.10pm from London. There were no direct trains on Sundays.

The stopping trains on the Badminton route almost all ran between Swindon and Bristol, until withdrawal in April 1961. There were five, weekdays only, initially, four in 1923, three in 1943 and two in 1961. There was a short working from Swindon in some years and extra trains called at Badminton.

Trains calling at Patchway and Pilning have been mostly working between Bristol and Cardiff, or beyond, and have been at fairly short intervals, except at Pilning.

The service from Swindon to Cardiff was irregular in steam days, with some trains running direct and others via Bristol. Similarly, some between Swindon and Bristol travelled via Badminton, instead of Bath. By 1963 there were eleven expresses taking the 1903 route to South Wales.

The first timetable after the opening of Bristol Parkway in 1972 showed only two Paddington - Bristol trains calling there, but there were 19 direct to Cardiff or beyond. The Sunday figure was nine.

From May 2002, the London-Cardiff service was updated to the best ever: a 30-minute interval on Mondays to Fridays and hourly at weekends.

The local services within Monmouthshire will be considered in a future volume.

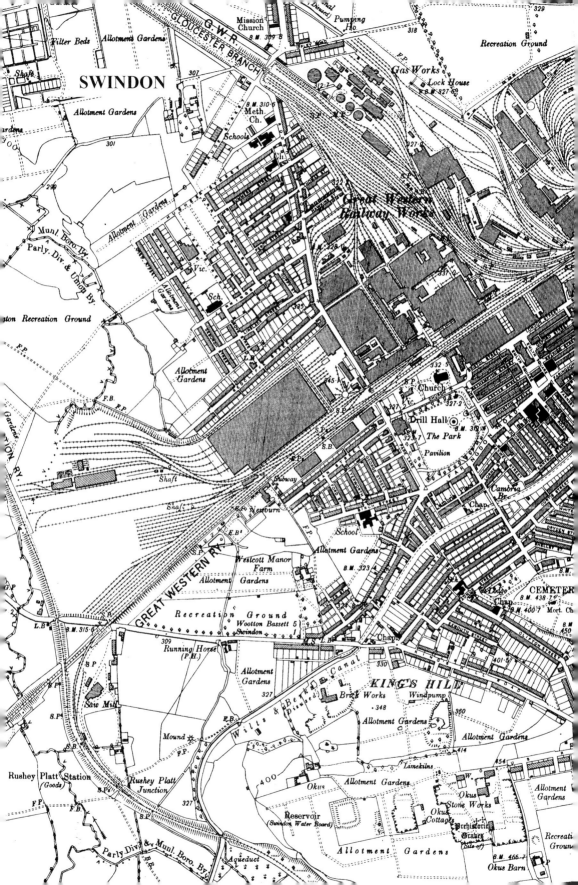

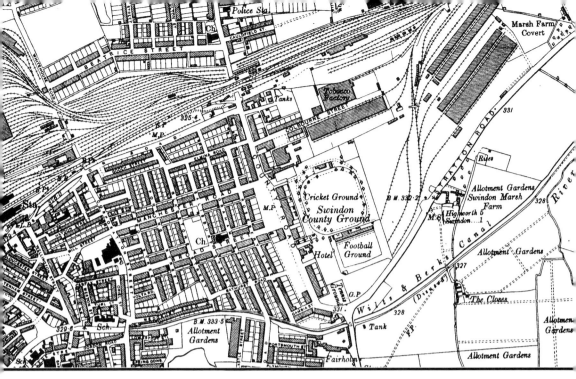

IV.　　The London to Bristol main line runs diagonally from right to left and the station is to the right of the join in this 1925 map. It came into use on 17th July 1842, by which time the GWR was beginning to plan its works. The map shows this almost at its optimum; it is illustrated in pictures 106 to 115 in our *Didcot to Swindon* album and was in use from 1843 until 1986. The north-south route on the left is that of the Midland & South Western Junction Railway which became part of the GWR in 1923 and is featured in our *Cheltenham to Andover* volume. The connecting curve was opened on 6th February 1882 and appears in picture 11 in *Swindon to Bristol*. The disused Wilts & Berks Canal runs across the map; it once brought coal here for the GWR.

1.　　The station was provided with two platforms and refreshment rooms from the outset. A subway was added in 1870, this being in addition to the footbridge which is seen from the west in this early 20th century view. (Lens of Sutton)

2.   A panorama from the east in 1921 includes a lengthy up milk train. Tank wagons would be used for this traffic from the next decade onwards. Note the massive finials on the gas lamps; the GWR had its own gasworks, which is on the left page of the map. (LGRP/NRM)

3.   After having worked coal trains from South Wales, a group of locos return there on Sunday 24th April 1955. They are nos 3851, 3866, 6389, 3818 and 5980 *Dingley Hall*. The footbridge was removed on 21st October 1962. (P.J.Kelley)

4.   Bay platforms were added in the 1870s, as traffic increased and broad gauge usage diminished. On the right are platforms 2 and 3. Out of view was No. 1, which was used by through local down trains. On the left is No. 5, the up main, and beyond the carriage shed and the up side building is No. 8, used by through up local trains. Bays 6 and 7 are in the distance. (Lens of Sutton)

5.	Class 4 4-6-0 stands at platform 2 on 15th April 1956 with the "Severn Venturer" railtour, the photographer giving us the opportunity to see platform 1 as well. At no. 4 is no. 5051 *Earl Bathurst* with a Paddington to South Wales excursion. That locomotive now resides at the Didcot Railway Centre. (F.Hornby)

6.	A four-wheeled railbus (no. W79978) stands at platform 6 on 17th September 1963; such units were used on the branches from Kemble. One of the Blue Pullmans speeds towards London, these trains being used from both Bristol and South Wales. (M.A.N.Johnston)

7.	The 18.00 Paddington to Swansea was hauled by D1053 *Western Patriarch* on 13th June 1966, soon after steam traction had been abolished. The two signal boxes were closed and replaced by a panel on 3rd March 1968. At the same time platform 5 became No. 3, and No. 8 was designated No. 1. East Box had 80 levers and West Box had 174. (J.Day)

8.   Most down trains used platform 3, this HST being an example on 6th April 1985. A DMU stands at platform 2, a bay created for Gloucester services terminating here. It is on the site of the carriage shed seen in picture no. 4. The buildings on the down side were demolished and replaced by a 12-storey office block, with the booking office on its ground floor, in the early 1970s. (C.L.Caddy)

9.   The former down main platform (right) was relegated to mail and parcel traffic, together with some football specials. However, it was extended and brought back into passenger use on 2nd June 2003. The 17.30 Paddington to Carmarthen HST is arriving on 14th August 1996. (M.J.Stretton)

WEST OF SWINDON

10.   Part of the Swindon Works and some of the scrap sidings are on the left of this 1953 panorama from the former MSWJR bridge over the main line. On the right is the end of the 1939 carriage shed, together with the 27-lever Rushey Platt signal box. Beyond it was Rodbourne Lane box, which had 31 levers; both closed in March 1968. The connecting curve on the right to Swindon Town was used by passenger trains in 1882-85 and 1923-61; it was closed totally in 1975. (H.F.Wheeller/R.S.Carpenter)

11.   Studley signal box had a nine-lever frame and was about five miles from Swindon. Passing it on 16th May 1952 with the up "Bristolian" is no. 18100, which was built by Metropolitan Vickers in 1951 and was in traffic for only 18 months. It was one of two experimental gas turbine locomotives. The crossover was taken out of use on 26th April 1953, when the box was closed. Signal boxes called "Hay Lane" had existed on three different sites to the east, between the 1870s and 1968. It controlled two goods loops from 1941 to 1964. (B.Hilton/M.J.Stretton coll.)

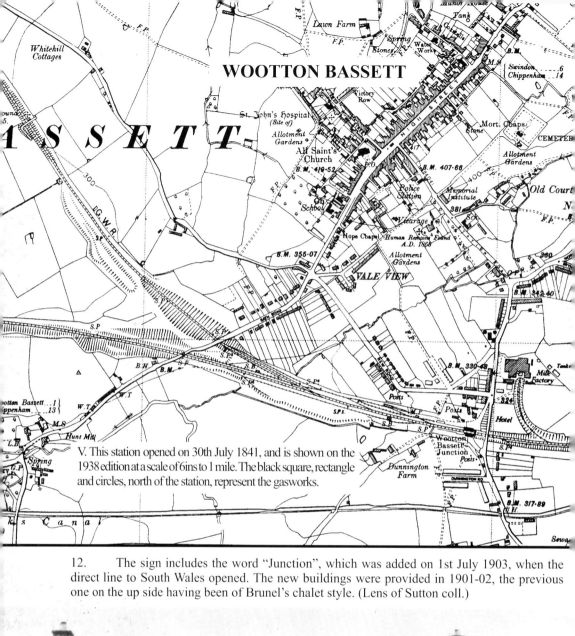

WOOTTON BASSETT

V. This station opened on 30th July 1841, and is shown on the 1938 edition at a scale of 6ins to 1 mile. The black square, rectangle and circles, north of the station, represent the gasworks.

12.   The sign includes the word "Junction", which was added on 1st July 1903, when the direct line to South Wales opened. The new buildings were provided in 1901-02, the previous one on the up side having been of Brunel's chalet style. (Lens of Sutton coll.)

13.   Approach roads were available on both sides of the station, the other being evident in the previous picture. The GWR was certainly generous with weather protection for passengers, unlike the operators of the present platform 2 at Swindon. (Lens of Sutton coll.)

14.   A view from the footbridge in 1931 includes milk vans in the dock and the down goods loop passing behind the 1902 East Box. This had a 57-lever frame. The base of the previous box can be seen at the end of the down platform. The loop lasted until 1966, when it became an engineers siding. (Brunel University/Mowat coll.)

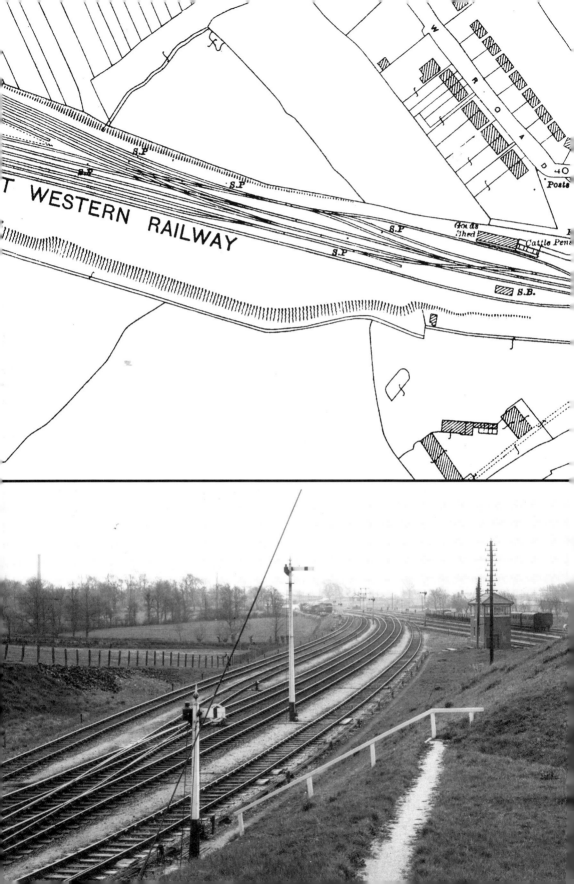

T WESTERN RAILWAY

S.P.

S.P.

S.P.

S.P.

S.P.

W R O A D

40

Posts

Goods Shed

Cattle Pens

S.B.

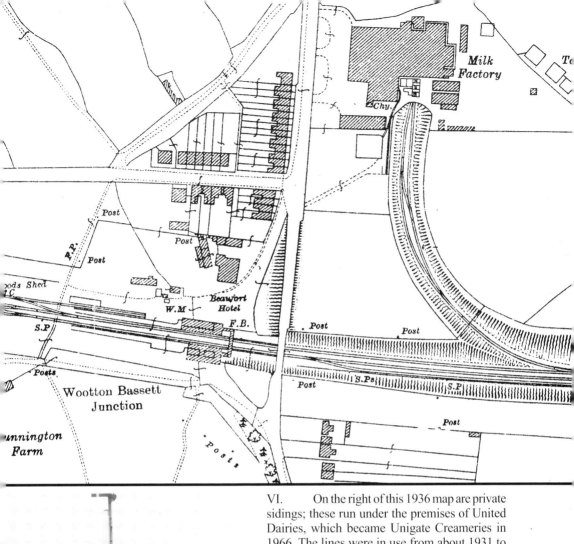

Milk
Factory

Chy.

Post

Post

Post

Post

R.P.

Post

oods Shed

W.M

Beaufort
Hotel

F.B.

Post

Post

S.P.

Posts

S.P.

Post

S.P.

Wootton Bassett
Junction

Post

Posts

unnington
Farm

VI.   On the right of this 1936 map are private sidings; these run under the premises of United Dairies, which became Unigate Creameries in 1966. The lines were in use from about 1931 to 1971, 30 tank wagons often being sent to London daily. South of the creamery is the down refuge siding, which was in place from around 1900 to 1953. The crane (marked C.) was of one-ton capacity.

15.   The 37-lever West Box features in this 1921 record; the companion box is in the distance. Both lasted until March 1968. On the left is "South Wales Up Goods Loop". The line parallel to it became a siding in 1966 and was removed in 1978. (LGRP/NRM)

16.   No. D855 speeds west on 21st October 1962 through the deserted station, which had a staff of over 20 in the 1930s and closed on 4th January 1965. The local population of about 5000 has doubled since that time and there has been agitation for the station to be reopened. (C.L.Caddy)

17.   Running onto the South Wales line on 8th June 1976 are nos 37142 and 37236 with empty hoppers destined for Tytherington Quarry in Gloucestershire. The junction was realigned in December 1978 to allow the speed limit to be raised from 50 to 70mph. The siding on the extreme right was used as a stone terminal by Foster Yeoman from January 1984. (G.Gillham)

Other views of this station can be found in *Swindon to Bristol* in pictures 12 to 16.

18.   No. 66009 stands on the up goods loop with a train loaded with coal for Didcot Power Station, while an HST approaches at speed from Bath. On the right is the site of the goods yard, which closed to general traffic on 19th May 1964. There has been reversible working to Swindon since 1981. (M.Turvey)

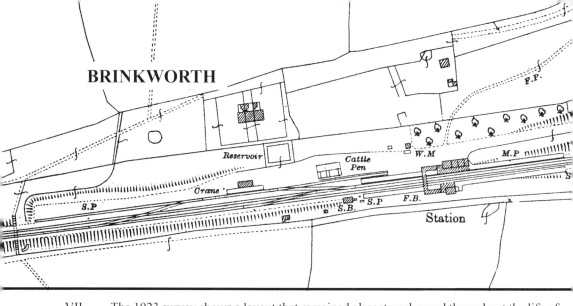

BRINKWORTH

Reservoir

Cattle Pen

Crane

W.M

M.P

S.P

S.B.

S.P

F.B.

Station

F.P.

VII.   The 1923 survey shows a layout that remained almost unchanged throughout the life of the station, which closed to all traffic on 3rd November 1961. Also marked is the crane, which was of 30cwt capacity, and the signal box (S.B.). This had 21 levers and closed on 15th March 1959. The crossovers were not used after 1958.

19.   A westward panorama from 1922 features one of the elegant tapered wooden signal posts and some of the many milk churns despatched daily. In 1910, 26,748 were loaded. There was usually a staff of five, but the post of station master was abolished in 1934. For many years, the service each way comprised four trains on weekdays and two on Sundays. The population was just over 1000 during the life of the station. (LGRP/NRM)

LITTLE SOMERFORD

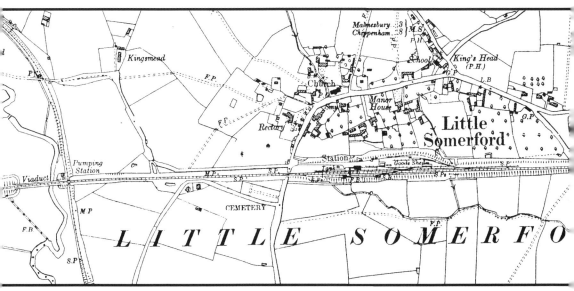

VIII.   The 1925 edition at 6ins to 1 mile has our route from right to left and the Malmesbury branch from Dauntsey passing under it. Provision of a curve linking the two in 1933 enabled branch trains to run from Little Somerford instead, from 17th July. The village housed only 323 in 1901; the entire 1903 route was thinly populated.

20.   The photographer is standing on the Malmesbury line which formed a third track parallel to the main lines as far as the point of divergence. This picture is from the 1930s, during which period there was a staff of six or seven. The loops were lengthened greatly in 1941 for wartime traffic. (LGRP/NRM)

21.	An up goods train takes water on 9th July 1959. The signal box had a 78-lever frame and was in use until 18th June 1967, the loops having been taken out of use in April 1966. The goods yard had cranes rated at one and six tons. Lighting by acetylene gas was introduced in 1939, the shed on the left probably housing the generator. (H.C.Casserley)

22.	Passenger service was withdrawn on 3rd April 1961 and goods followed on 10th June 1963. This view is from a down train in 1961; until April 1956, such trains could cross directly to the branch line, which closed to passengers on 10th September 1951 and completely on 12th November 1962. (A.E.Bennett)

WEST OF LITTLE SOMERFORD

23.   The 150yd long Somerford Viaduct is shown on the left of the map. The Malmesbury branch passed under the right hand of it, just out of view. (A.E.Bennett)

> **The Malmesbury branch and Little Somerford are featured in our _Branch Lines of West Wiltshire._**

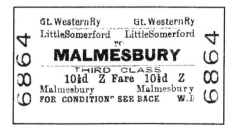

HULLAVINGTON

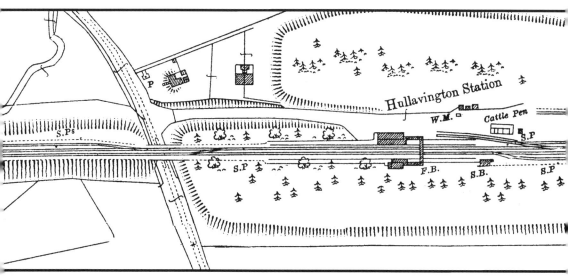

IX.   The 1923 survey includes the refuge sidings which were both extended to form loops in July 1941, to speed up wartime traffic. The new points were electrically worked from a hand-operated generator in the signal box. There were under 900 souls in the parish during the life of the station.

24.   In the background is the goods shed, adjacent to which was a 30cwt crane. Initially the staff comprised a station master, two porters and two signalmen. The last four worked shifts; a lorry driver was added later, as was a third signalman so that the box could be manned all night. (Lens of Sutton coll.)

25.   The down loop was also extended westward in 1941, to run behind the down platform (right). The trees of 1903 are in this 1922 photograph. Over 9000 milk churns were handled here back in 1910. Passenger traffic ceased on 3rd April 1961. (LGRP/NRM)

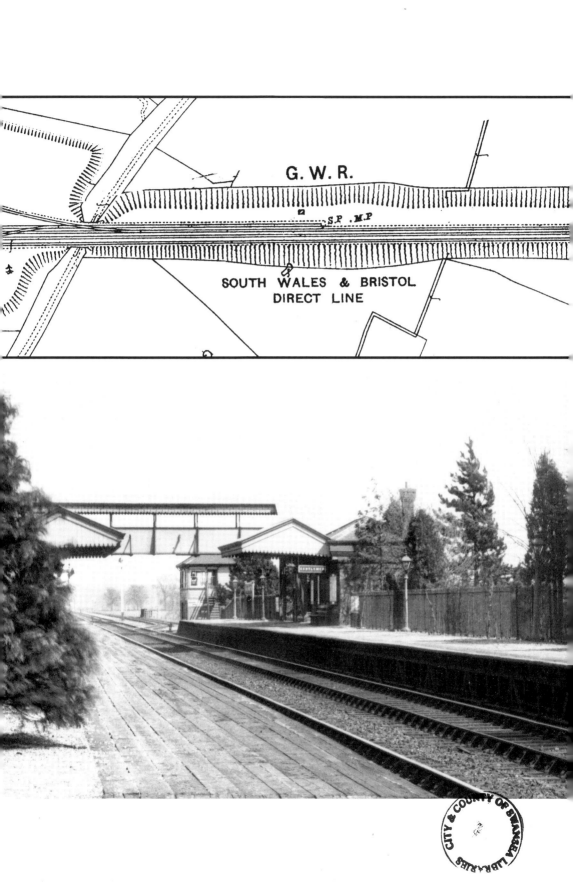

G. W. R.

SP .MP

SOUTH WALES & BRISTOL
DIRECT LINE

26.　　Two long sidings were added on the north side of the goods yard and these were retained by the engineers long after freight service was withdrawn on 4th October 1965. The 39-lever signal box was closed on 24th March 1968, but the loops were retained. (R.M.Casserley)

Hullavington	1903	1913	1923	1933
Passenger tickets issued	2316	3902	3510	1692
Season tickets issued	*	*	4	1
General goods forwarded (tons)	671	1250	729	410
Coal and coke received (tons)	506	1368	1583	999
Other minerals received (tons)	1115	3627	674	108
General goods received (tons)	721	1897	1838	517
Trucks of livestock handled	19	63	42	32

(* not available.)

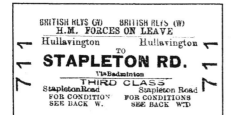

WEST OF HULLAVINGTON

27.   No. D1039 *Western King* is about to take an up express under an unusual iron aqueduct on 26th March 1964. The next feature westward is Alderton Tunnel, which is 506 yds long. (M.A.N.Johnston)

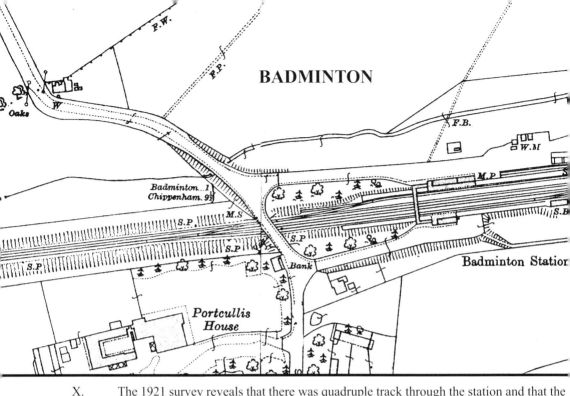

BADMINTON

Badminton Station

X.   The 1921 survey reveals that there was quadruple track through the station and that the sidings were longer than those at the other 1903 stations visited so far. Portcullis House was a hotel "in 9 acres affording maximum comfort for Hunting Quarters".

28.   A down freight was included in this view from about 1910, in which year 15,440 milk churns were despatched. There was a staff of 10 to 14 in the 1920s. Goods services began on 1st January 1903 from the east and on 1st May 1903 from the west. (Lens of Sutton coll.)

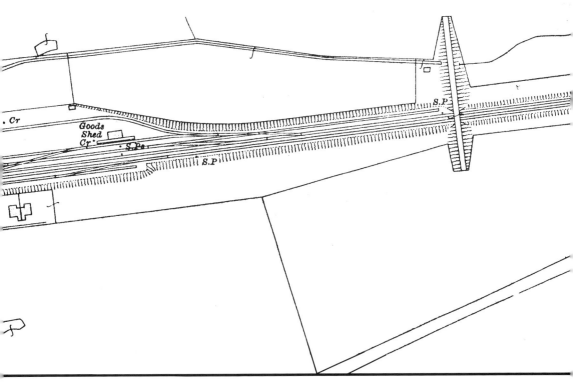

29.   The up side buildings (centre in this 1959 picture) had been extended eastward in 1947 by more than 50%, to increase parcel and cycle accommodation. The Duke of Beaufort of Badminton House had demanded that his coat of arms was incorporated in the west elevation and that four trains stopped here daily. It was annulment of this covenant that delayed closure until 3rd June 1968. (R.M.Casserley)

30. There was road access to both sides of the station; this is the down side in 1959. In the background is the goods yard, which closed on 1st November 1966. It had two cranes, their capacities being 30cwt and 6 tons. The nearest village was Acton Turville and this had under 300 residents. (H.C.Casserley)

31. The Duke had demanded that some expresses stopped here, but in 1964 there were only two up trains: the 9.27am and 5.27pm (on Sundays there was only one). All originated at Swansea and this is one of them. Prior to the demise of local trains in April 1961, there were two other fast trains to Paddington, plus two stopping trains to Swindon. (Stations UK)

32.   Another 1964 photograph and this has the down loop on the left; this lasted until 1st November 1970. The up loop and the 61-lever signal box were taken out of use on 10th May 1971. The latter was to the left of the camera. The buildings on the right were still standing in 2003, as was the goods shed. The entire 1903 route east of Westerleigh Junction was closed for upgrading from 5th May to 6th October 1986 in readiness for HSTs to run at up to 125mph. (Stations UK)

WEST OF BADMINTON

33.   After passing through the 4444yd long Sodbury Tunnel, trains entered a cutting which was deliberately created level to accommodate water troughs, the only ones on the 1903 route. The water came from the infant River Frome, which flooded the line on 23rd December 1911, covering the rails but not the troughs. The level section has been inclined since the troughs were removed in 1964. The aqueduct was raised one foot on 7th September 1986 and the river banks were strengthened to reduce flood risk. (P.Q.Treloar coll.)

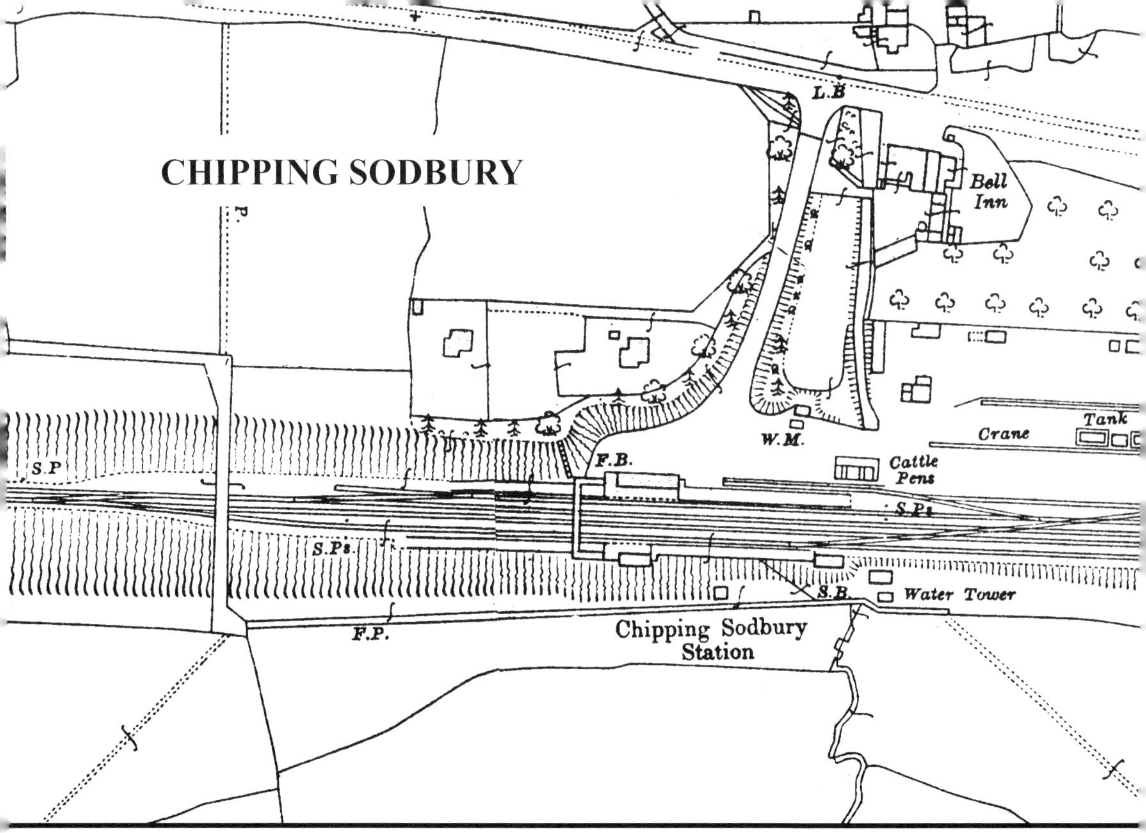
CHIPPING SODBURY
L.B
Bell
Inn
W.M.
F.B.
Cattle
Pens
Crane
Tank
S.P
S.Ps
S.Ps.
S.B.
Water Tower
F.P.
Chipping Sodbury
Station

XI. Probably the busiest station on the new route, the 1921 map shows road access only from the north. The wagon weighing machine (W.M.) was originally a 12-ton model. It was increased to 20 tons in 1954 and later to 60 tons, stone from Arnold Quarries being the main commodity weighed.

34. An early postcard shows the view west soon after completion of the station, when there was a staff of ten. To allow construction of the line, eight cottages had to be demolished in this district. This was the most populous place on the new route: 1177 in 1901 and 2439 in 1961. (Lens of Sutton coll.)

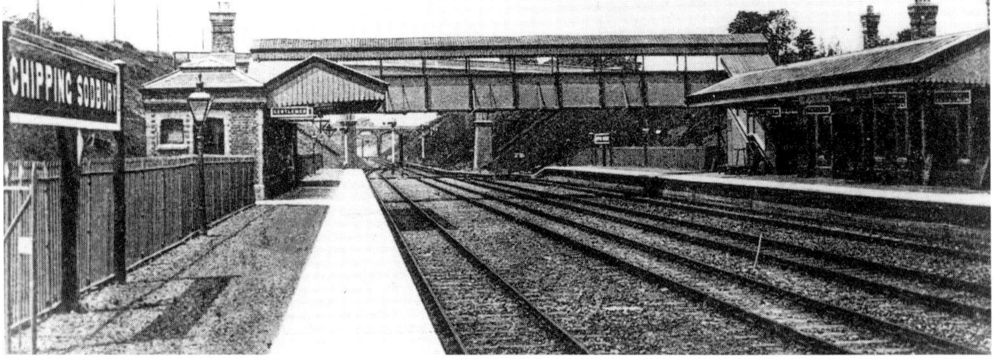
CHIPPING SODBURY

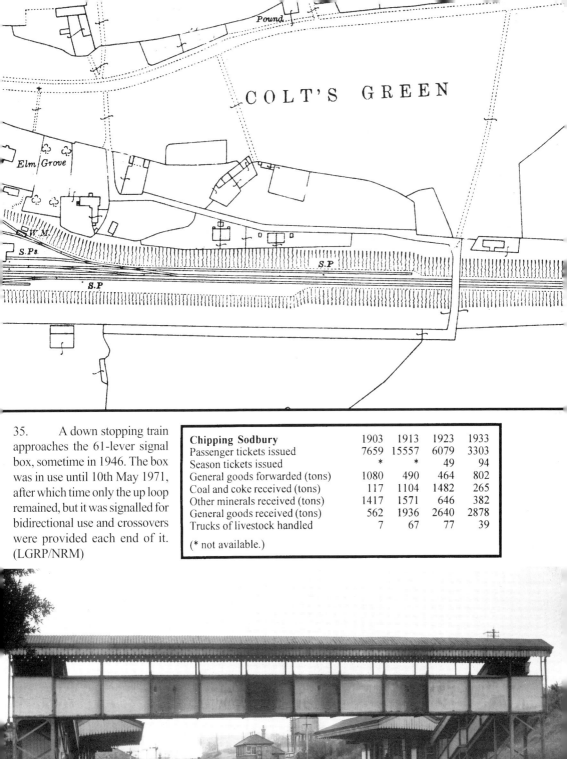

35.　A down stopping train approaches the 61-lever signal box, sometime in 1946. The box was in use until 10th May 1971, after which time only the up loop remained, but it was signalled for bidirectional use and crossovers were provided each end of it. (LGRP/NRM)

Chipping Sodbury	1903	1913	1923	1933
Passenger tickets issued	7659	15557	6079	3303
Season tickets issued	*	*	49	94
General goods forwarded (tons)	1080	490	464	802
Coal and coke received (tons)	117	1104	1482	265
Other minerals received (tons)	1417	1571	646	382
General goods received (tons)	562	1936	2640	2878
Trucks of livestock handled	7	67	77	39

(* not available.)

36.   No. 7923 *Speke Hall* tears through with an up express in September 1956. Both loops had been extended in 1912 and the up one was lengthened eastwards in January 1943 to form an up goods loop. Passenger service was withdrawn on 3rd April 1961, but the goods yard remained open until 20th June 1966. (R.S.Carpenter)

37.   Shunting in the yard was recorded on 26th March 1964 from a position overlooking the catch point of the down refuge siding. As elsewhere, the yard had cranes rated at 6 tons and 30cwt capacity. Most of the sidings were retained by the engineers and were still in place in 2000. (M.A.N.Johnston)

38.   Pictured on the same day was no. D1002 *Western Explorer* with an up express. The deserted platform had received 10,024 milk churns back in 1910. The route had been engineered for high speed running. (M.A.N.Johnston)

39.   Seen from the remains of the up platform on 18th March 1997 is no. 60078, hauling a load of imported coal from Avonmouth, destined for Didcot Power Station. Down trains using the loop are controlled by the two signals on the right. Both main lines could be used in either direction since 1986. (M.J.Stretton)

WEST OF CHIPPING SODBURY

40.   Bound for Swansea on 26th March 1964 is no. D1008 *Western Harrier*. It is passing Westerleigh East signal box, which had 44 levers and opened on 1st July 1942, along with the two loops and four sidings that were laid on the left to serve twelve wartime sidings. In the background is Wapley Common box (59 levers), which came into use on the same day and lasted until 18th July 1965, although the lines to Wapley Common Depot were usable until May 1967. Westerleigh East functioned until 10th May 1971. (M.A.N.Johnston)

XII.   The 1922 survey at 6ins to 1 mile has the original Westerleigh East box on the right, its dates in use being 1st May 1903 to 4th February 1907, 9th March 1908 to 18th December 1916 and 18th February 1919 to 10th July 1927. The curve was open again between 16th August 1942 and 4th January 1950, but the box was then ¼-mile further east. West Junction box (23 levers) was in use from 1st May 1903 to 10th May 1971, when Bristol Panel took over. All Gloucester to Bristol trains used the route westwards from 3rd January 1970 and the line to the south was taken over by the engineers as far as Mangotsfield. Part of it later served a refuse terminal and an oil depot, the single line still being in use in 2004. The presence of shafts is explained in the next map caption.

Nibley

National
Concrete Slab Factory

Yate
Station

Eggshill Common

Swan Inn

TRAMWAY

Quarry

S.B

S.P

S.P

Yate
Chemical Works

M.P

B.8

Mail
Apparatus

S.P

WESTERLEIGH COMMON

G.W.R.

YATE BRANCH

shaft 200

F.P

P.P

F.R.

S.P

S.P

Beech Hill

Old
Quarry

Old Quarry

S.P

Say's
Wood

Old
Air Shaft

BRISTOL & BIRMINGHAM M.R.

Rodford

Rodfordhill
Farm

G.P
L.B

Elm Farm

W

S.P

Westerleigh
North Junction

M.P
S.B

F.R.

S.P

F.P

M.P

Post

G.W.R.

WESTERLEIGH LOOP

G.W.R.

YATE BRANCH

S.P

Westerle
East June

S.Pt

S.B

Congregational
Church

S.Pt

S.P

B.S

Rises

S.B

S.P.

W

S.P.

M.P

Dodmoor Farm

S.P

Westerleigh
West Junction

Vicarage

B.S

Be m

COUNTY OF

Grove Farm

W

Old Quarry

Copp Hill

41.　　Westerleigh North Junction was photographed on 2nd July 1960, as no. 5912 *Queen's Hall* rounds the curve with a Weston-super-Mare to Birmingham Snow Hill express. The curve on the left and the signal box had been closed since 1950. (M.A.N.Johnston)

42.　　Seen on the same day is West Box, with an Ilfracombe to Wolverhampton train about to pass behind it. The down line from Swindon is in the foreground. (M.A.N.Johnston)

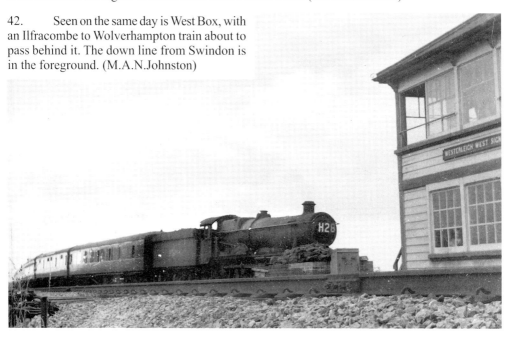

Coalpit Heath	1913	1923	1933
Passenger tickets issued	13389	4911	2425
Season tickets issued	-	74	75
Coal forwarded	34327	31769	29962
General goods forwarded (tons)	254	40	45
Coal and coke received (tons)	59	132	-
Other minerals received (tons)	366	193	98
General goods received (tons)	1042	972	636
Trucks of livestock handled	-	-	1
(* not available.)			

Other views of this location can be found in our *Gloucester to Bristol* album.

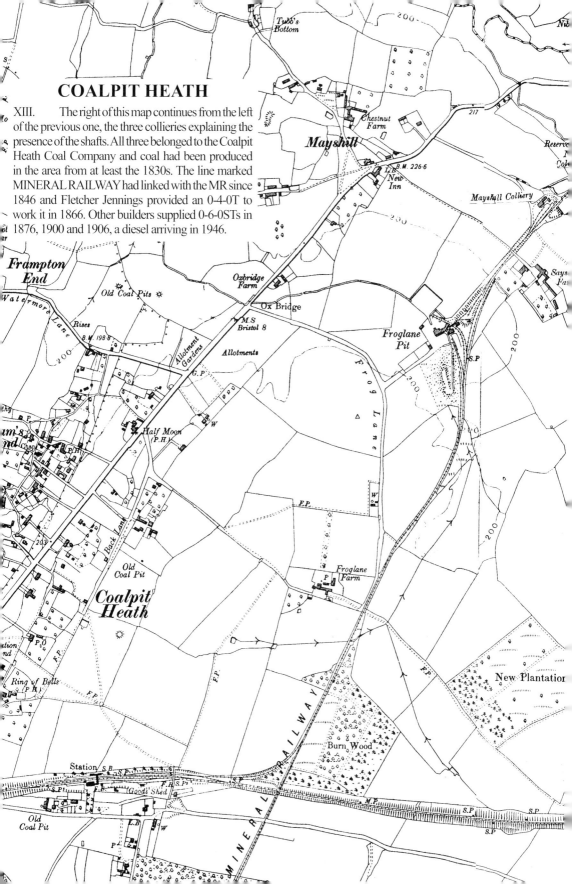

COALPIT HEATH

XIII.   The right of this map continues from the left of the previous one, the three collieries explaining the presence of the shafts. All three belonged to the Coalpit Heath Coal Company and coal had been produced in the area from at least the 1830s. The line marked MINERAL RAILWAY had linked with the MR since 1846 and Fletcher Jennings provided an 0-4-0T to work it in 1866. Other builders supplied 0-6-0STs in 1876, 1900 and 1906, a diesel arriving in 1946.

Tubb's Bottom

Chestnut Farm

Mayshill

L.B. New Inn

B.M. 226·6

Reservo

Mayshill Colliery

Frampton End

Oxbridge Farm

Ox Bridge

Watermore Lane

Rises

B.M. 198·8

M.S. Bristol 8

Old Coal Pits

Allotment Gardens

Allotments

G.P.

Froglane Pit

S.P.

Frog Lane

Says Fa

Half Moon (P.H.)

W

Chap.

m's nd

P.H.

Back Lane

Old Coal Pit

203

F.P.

W

F.P.

Coalpit Heath

Froglane Farm

New Plantatio

P.O.

Ring of Bells (P.H.)

F.P.

F.P.

F.P.

Burn Wood

Station

S.B.

S.P.

F.

S.P.

Good's Shed

S.P.

Old Coal Pit

L.B.

P.

MINERAL RAILWAY

M.P.

S.P.

S.P.

S.P.

43.	A 1949 eastward panorama includes wagons standing in the colliery exchange sidings. The 33-lever signal box (left) closed on 7th June 1964, the loops having been taken up a few months earlier. The footbridge in the distance is still in use; the next two views are from it. (LGRP/NRM)

44.	No. 5051 *Earl Bathurst* (now preserved) speeds west with "The South Wales Pullman" in October 1956. The colliery lines had recently been removed from the land on the left. (R.S.Carpenter)

45.   An up local train included two Eastern Region teak-panelled coaches on 2nd July 1960; they were hauled by no. 1024 *County of Pembroke*. All local traffic here ceased on 3rd April 1961. There was only a one-ton crane provided. (M.A.N.Johnston)

46.   The bridge carrying the main line over the mineral railway was photographed in 1960, several years after the last coal had passed under it. The National Coal Board had closed Frog Lane Pit and Mayshill Colliery by 1949, the other mine having a siding until about 1953. (M.A.N.Johnston)

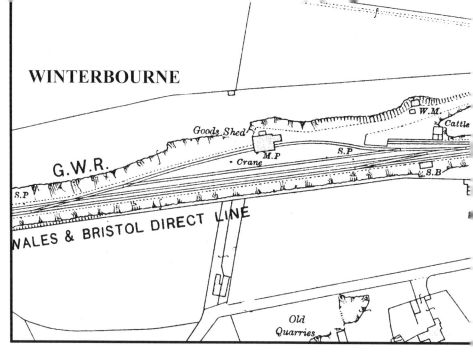

WINTERBOURNE

XIV.   The road between Winterbourne Down and Watleys End is at the join of the pages of this 1920 map. It passes over the line between the station and the goods yard. The former closed on 3rd April 1961 and the latter on 7th October 1963. On the right is Hackford Viaduct, which is 269yds in length.

47.   There was a staff of five or six in the 1920s. This westward view from the 1950s has, in the distance, the goods yard and the signal box. The latter had 27 levers and closed on 7th June 1970. For many years it was switched out and only manned in the mornings. (C.G.Maggs)

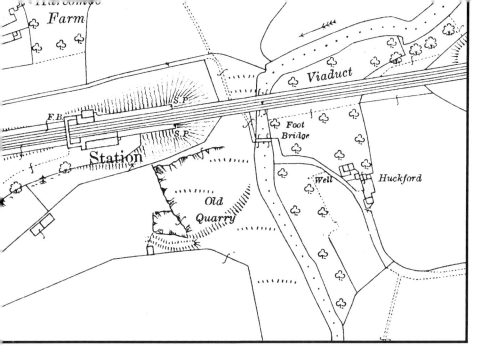

48.   Looking west on 9th May 1964, we witness the demise of the goods yard. The six-ton crane is evident, but the 50cwt one is not. The dock on the right once accommodated cattle pens. The crossover remained until the signal box closed. (P.J.Garland/R.S.Carpenter)

STOKE GIFFORD

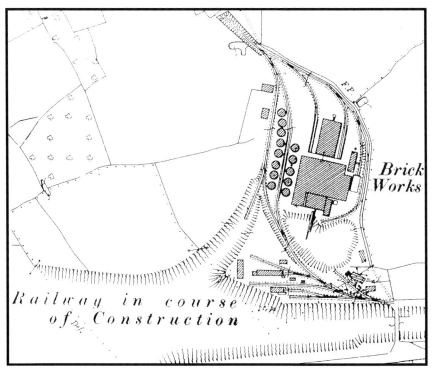

Brick
Works

Railway in course
of Construction

XV.   The contractor for construction of the new line was S.Pearson & Son Ltd and the firm established several brickworks along its 33½ mile length. This was the biggest and was surveyed in about 1898. It could produce up to 250,000 bricks per week and about 50m were used on the route. Its construction employed 4000 men, 17 steam excavators, 11 steam cranes and about 50 locomotives.

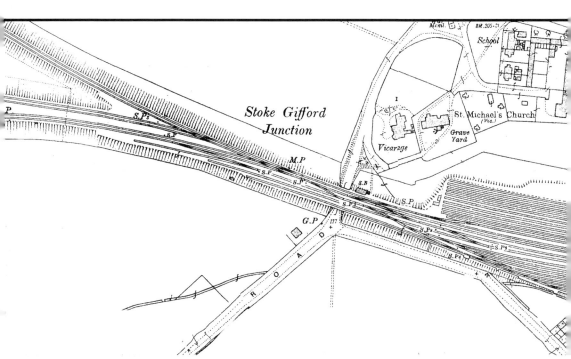

Stoke Gifford
Junction

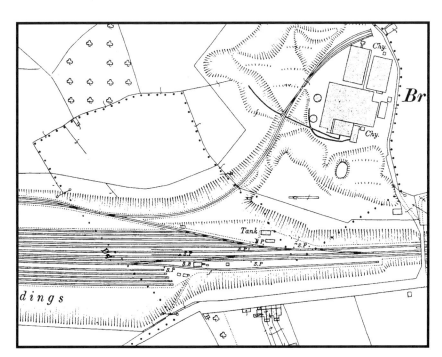

XVI.   Beaufort Brickworks passed from Pearsons to Pugsley & Sons in 1917 and is seen on the 1915 edition. Five sidings and a goods loop were laid each side of the main line, their principal purpose being to allow short coal trains from South Wales to be marshalled into long ones for the journey on the easier gradients eastwards. The maps are at a reduced scale.

XVII.   The 1935 edition includes the extra five sidings added each side in 1918 in response to traffic increase. The loop on the north side was used for brick traffic and the two sidings nearby were added in 1920 for cripples. Near the vicarage is West box. The centre pair of tracks on the left opened on 9th May 1910, the others opening with the new route in 1903.

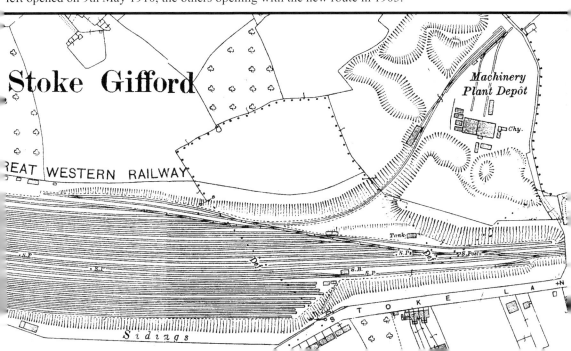

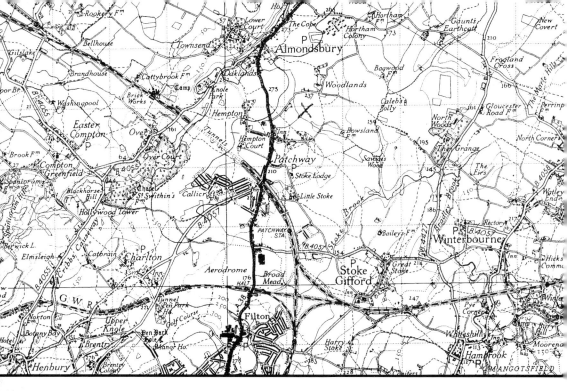

XVIII.   The 1946 map at 1ins to 1 mile has our route running from Winterbourne (right) to Pilning (top left). At the bottom (centre) is the line to Bristol, while the direct route westward to Avonmouth is left (lower). This ceased to have a regular passenger service on 23rd November 1964, but the embankment shown curving northwards from it received a single goods line on 22nd February 1971.

49.   No. 5322 approaches the yard with a down freight, sometime in 1961. It is viewed from the bridge to the brickworks. Slip coaches for Bristol from the 8.45am and 8.0pm Paddington to Fishguard Harbour expresses were detached in this vicinity from 22nd May 1923. The 2-6-0 was built in 1917 and is now at the Didcot Railway Centre. (P.Q.Treloar coll.)

50. A panorama from the other side of the bridge in 1964 includes Stoke Gifford East box, which had 31 levers and closed on 21st February 1971 when the yard ceased to be used for marshalling. (P.J.Garland/ R.S.Carpenter)

51. A further westward view features the down side of the yard. Extensive excavation was necessary to ensure a level area on which to stand unbraked trains. The 70-lever West box is in the distance; its life was the same as that of East box. Its larger lever frame was due to it controlling the junction for Bristol and South Wales trains. (C.G.Maggs)

52. From the same position as picture 50, this photo from 26th June 2003 shows EWS no. 66221 running through with imported coal from Avonmouth, bound for Didcot. On the right is the Royal Mail terminal, which was not used after 10th January 2004, and the up goods loop. The down goods loop and seven sidings are on the left. The latter were used by EWS for wagon repairs. (M.Turvey)

BRISTOL PARKWAY

53.   A new station was opened near the centre of the marshalling yard site on 1st July 1972 and two through goods lines were retained each side of it. It was photographed three months before opening. (British Railways)

54.   Facilities were modern, functional and minimal. Its assets included fast trains to London, the South West, South Wales and the Midlands, also proximity to motorways and North Bristol. (D.Thompson)

55.   An extensive free car park was provided and traffic developed quickly. Filton aircraft hangars are in the left background, while in the centre is Stoke Gifford Junction. No. 47520 departs with the 10.40 Taunton to Manchester on 16th October 1981, while nos 37241 and 37135 have just run round empty wagons on their way from Swindon to Tytherington, near Yate. (G.Gillham)

56.   Improved shelters were provided on the up platform at this exposed location. No. 47022 was recorded at the up platform on 5th May 1982, while attached to the High Speed Track Recording Coach and an empty train. (T.Heavyside)

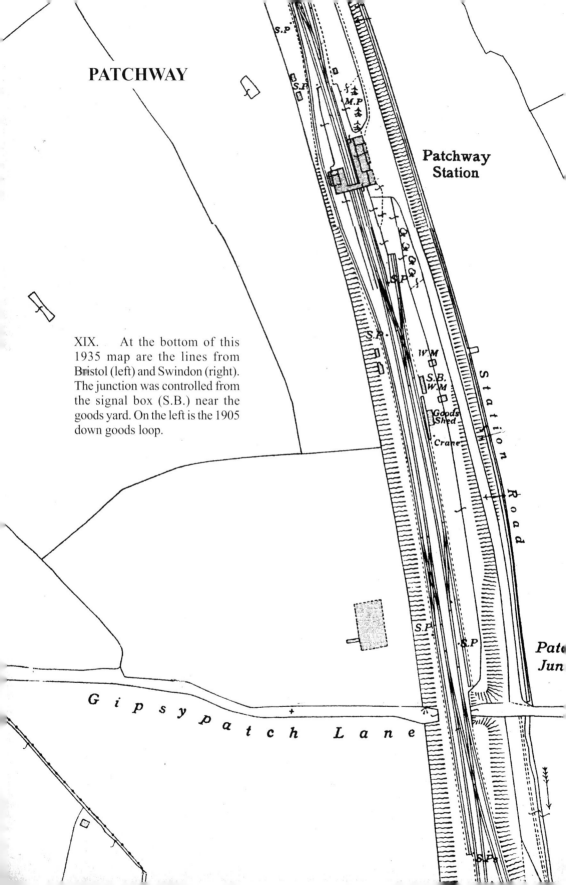

PATCHWAY

Patchway
Station

XIX.   At the bottom of this
1935 map are the lines from
Bristol (left) and Swindon (right).
The junction was controlled from
the signal box (S.B.) near the
goods yard. On the left is the 1905
down goods loop.

S.P

S.P

M.P

S.P

S.P

S.P

W.M

S.B.
W.M

Goods
Shed

Crane

S t a t i o n   R o a d

S.P

S.P

Pat
Jun

G i p s y p a t c h   L a n e

S.P

57.　　The rear of this up train is on the incline up from the Severn Tunnel, while the front part is on level track. The first station was ¼-mile north of the present one and had a passing loop, plus two sidings. The down line was the original single line to New Passage and was in use as such from 1863 to 1886, when the branch closed. This is one of the 3521 class 4-4-0s, rebuilt many times from a tank engine design of 1888. (Lens of Sutton)

58.　　The three ringed signal arms were for trains on the goods loops. A "Hall" class 4-6-0 is about to start the long descent to the tunnels with a mixture of GWR and SR coaches, probably from Portsmouth, in about 1949. (R.S.Carpenter)

59.	An up freight rattles under the fully enclosed footbridge of Patchway's second station, which opened on 10th August 1885 as "Patchway & Stoke Gifford". The suffix was dropped on 27th October 1908. The 2-8-2T no. 7202 from 1934 is now a resident of the Didcot Railway Centre. (P.Q.Treloar coll.)

60.	This southward view from the 1960s includes the goods yard, which closed on 5th July 1965, and the 45-lever signal box, which was in use until 22nd February 1971. The boxes to the north were Patchway Tunnel (8 levers - 29th August 1918 to 19th January 1965) and Cattybrook Siding (12 levers - 17th July 1881 to 22nd February 1971). The siding served a brickworks on the east side of the line. (Lens of Sutton coll.)

61.	The station was unstaffed from 14th October 1968 and the buildings were demolished soon after. The junction signal can be seen on the left as the down "South Wales Pullman" speeds north on 16th April 1973, destination Swansea. These eight-car diesel units were withdrawn three weeks later. Note the differing track levels, the new line being at a more uniform gradient. (G.Gillham)

62.	The station is in the background as nos 25054 and 25064 take empty bitumen tankers from Cranmore to Ellesmere Port on 4th May 1983. They will soon pass through two tunnels: Patchway Old (1246yds) and Patchway Short (62yds). By 2003, the station had a basic hourly service, but less on Sundays. (T.Heavyside)

63.   Nearer the station, but back in time, "Dukedog" 4-4-0 no. 9023 hauls a load of coal from South Wales. On the right is the up refuge siding, which was usable until 5th May 1968. (P.Q.Treloar coll.)

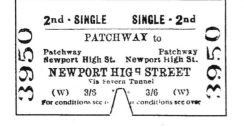

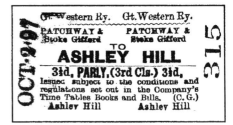

64.   A good clean exhaust was being created by no. 6021 *King Richard II* as it climbed on the new line at 1 in 100. Much of the old line (left) was at 1 in 90. (P.Q. Treloar coll.)

65.   No. 33027 was working the 12.15 Cardiff to Portsmouth Harbour on 4th May 1981. It is emerging from Patchway New Tunnel, which is one mile in length. (T. Heavyside)

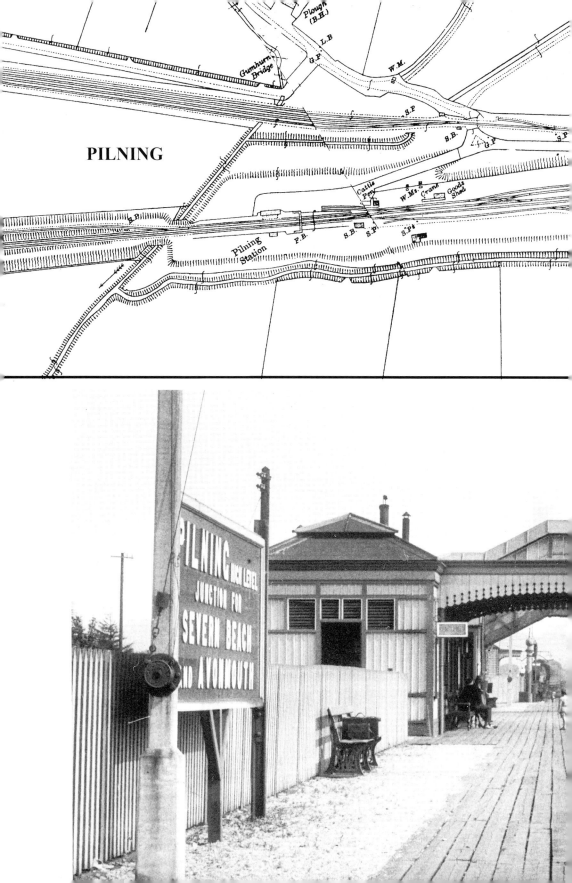

PILNING

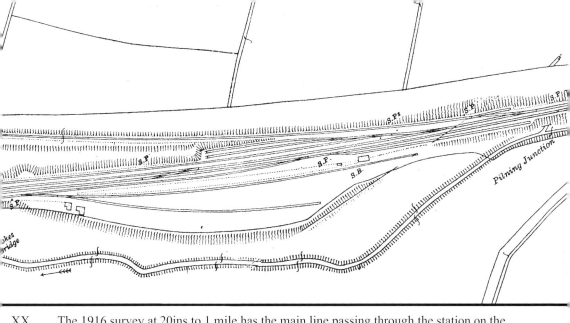

XX.   The 1916 survey at 20ins to 1 mile has the main line passing through the station on the left page. Above it is the single line route from Severn Beach, which opened on 5th February 1900. It was on the alignment of the New Passage branch. Pilning Low Level station was built nearby and was in use from 1928 until 1964.

66.   A 1930 eastward panorama includes a train in the 1905 down goods loop, the up one being completed in 1906. This station opened on 1st December 1886 and superseded the one on the branch. Double track to Patchway was completed on 27th May 1887. (LGRP/NRM)

CONVEYANCE OF MOTOR CARS AND MOTOR CYCLES THROUGH THE SEVERN TUNNEL

The following arrangements are available for the conveyance of motor cars and motor cycles accompanying Passengers by passenger train through the Severn Tunnel.

A quantity of petrol (not exceeding one quart in the case of motor cycles) may be left in the tanks, provided that—

(a) in the case of vehicles with gravity or autovac feed, the flow of petrol to the carburettor has been stopped by means of the shut-off cock provided.

(b) in the case of vehicles with electric petrol pump, the flow of petrol to the carburettor be interrupted by switching off the electric pump (switch key, if fitted, must be removed).

(c) with cars fitted with mechanical petrol pumps, the engine is stopped and the ignition key removed.

(d) the motor is free from the leakage of petrol.

Motor cycles are conveyed by ordinary trains booked to call at the stations named.

Cars are conveyed by the services shown below, and open carriage trucks are kept on hand at the stations for the purpose.

Cars should arrive at the stations in sufficient time to admit of loading 20 minutes before the train is due to depart. Prior advice by letter, telegram or telephone to the station is advisable (Severn Tunnel Junction—Tel. : Caldicot 210) (Pilning—Tel. : Pilning 6).

Waterproof sheets are provided to cover cars conveyed, at a charge of 1s. 7d. per sheet.

The following are the rates between Pilning and Severn Tunnel Junction under this arrangement:

	Severn Tunnel Jn. & Pilning
	Single
Motor Cars:	s. d.
At Owner's risk—	
Not exceeding 8 H.P. ...	8 2
Exceeding 8 H.P.	9 10
Motor Cycles (loaded in Guard's Van), accompanied at Railway Executive's risk:	
Not exceeding 120lbs. ...	1 11
120 to 200 lbs.	2 5
Above 200 lbs.	3 1
Side Cars (loaded in Guard's Van), accompanied at Railway Executive's risk:	
With 1 seat	2 5
With 2 or more seats ...	3 7

When the side car is not detached from a motor cycle a special truck is necessary, and the charge is as for a motor car.

TRAIN SERVICE

	Week Days			Sundays	
	a.m.	p.m.	p.m.	a.m.	p.m.
Pilning (H. Level) dep.	10J15	6 38	8 55	9 K48	9 48
Severn Tunnel Jn. arr.	10J27	6 52	9 8	10 K2	10 2

	Week Days			Sundays	
	a.m.	p.m.	p.m.	a.m.	p.m.
Severn Tunnel Jn. dep.	9J15	2 34	6 55	9 K16	9 16
Pilning (H. Level) arr.	9J27	2 48	7 10	9 K28	9 30

J—Mondays and Saturdays only.

K—Runs 3rd, 10th, 17th, and 24th October, 19th and 26th December, 1948, 2nd January, 1949, and commencing 17th, April, 1949.

PASSENGER FARES

Severn Tunnel Junction and Pilning:

(Single) 1st Class, 5s. 2d. ; 3rd Class, 3s. 1d

BEACHLEY — AUST FERRY — RIVER SEVERN

AUGUST 1966

A Half-Hourly Service will operate from Beachley and Aust Piers from :

(Broken lines denote breaks in service from low or high water)

		a.m.						p.m.
1	Mon.	9.00	until	2.00 p.m.	——	4.30 p.m.	until	7.30
2	Tue.	9.00	,,	2.30 p.m.	——	5.00 p.m.	,,	7.30
3	Wed.	9.00	,,	3.00 p.m.	——	5.30 p.m.	,,	7.30
4	Thu.	9.00	,,	3.30 p.m.	——	6.00 p.m.	,,	7.30
5	Fri.	9.00	,,	4.00 p.m.	——	6.30 p.m.	,,	7.30
6	Sat.	9.00	,,	4.30 p.m.	——	7.00 p.m.	,,	7.30
7	Sun.	9.00			until			5.00
8	Mon.	8.30			,,			5.30
9	Tue.	9.00			,,			6.00
10	Wed.	9.00			,,			7.00
11	Thu.	9.00			,,			7.30
12	Fri.	9.00	until	9.30 a.m.	——	11.00 a.m.	until	7.30
13	Sat.	9.00	,,	10.30 a.m.	——	12.00 noon	,,	7.30
14	Sun.	9.00	,,	11.30 a.m.	——	2.00 p.m.	,,	7.30
15	Mon.	8.30	,,	12.30 p.m.	——	3.00 p.m.	,,	7.30
16	Tue.	9.00	,,	1.30 p.m.	——	4.30 p.m.	,,	7.30
17	Wed.	9.30	,,	2.30 p.m.	——	5.30 p.m.	.,	7.30
18	Thu.	10.30	,,	3.00 p.m.	——	6.30 p.m.	,,	7.30
19	Fri.	11.30			until			4.00
20	Sat.	9.00	until	10.00 a.m.	——	12.00 noon	,,	4.30
21	Sun.	9.00			until			5.30
22	Mon.	8.30			,,			6.00
23	Tue.	9.00			,,			6.30
24	Wed.	9.00			,,			7.30
25	Thu.	9.00			,,			7.30
26	Fri.	9.00			,,			7.30
27	Sat.	9.00	until	11.00 a.m.	——	12.30 p.m.	until	7.30
28	Sun.	9.00	,,	12.00 noon	——	2.00 p.m.	,,	7.30
29	Mon.	8.30	,,	1.00 p.m.	——	3.30 p.m.	,,	7.30
30	Tue.	9.00	,,	1.30 p.m.	——	4.00 p.m.	,,	7.30
31	Wed.	9.00	,,	2.00 p.m.	——	5.00 p.m.	,,	7.30

XXI.   The GWR introduced a car-carrying service through the Severn Tunnel in 1910, but this was suspended during World War I. It was reintroduced in 1921 and cars would be "conveyed by ordinary trains booked to call at Severn Tunnel Junction, Pilning and Patchway, and a supply of petrol is available at these stations". All fuel tanks had to be drained and the GWR refilled them with the same amount at the end of the journey. British Railways did not make this demand and offered up to three dedicated trains daily each way. The fee was a massive 42s 6d in 1924, but it was reduced to 5s 0d for small cars (6s 0d for large) from March 1933, with passengers extra. The locomotive was usually a 2-6-2T and the wagons were four-wheelers. In the final years, bogie carflats and a retired slip coach were hauled by a Type 3 diesel. The Severn Bridge opened on 8th September 1966 and the service was withdrawn on 6th October following. The tunnel timetable for 1948 is shown, along with that for the alternative means of crossing the Severn. Its problems included the tidal intervals shown, the weather and queuing for an hour or two, by which time the service might be suspended for one of the other reasons. Thus the train could be a better option, if one of the infrequent trips was due.

67.   A loaded train is about to depart, probably in the 1920s. The car on the left is a Bean 11hp Brougham of 1924. Passengers were involved in more shunting on journeys to Wales. (G.Nichols coll.)

68.　　　No. 6834 *Dummer Grange* passes through with a down freight, while empties stand on the down goods loop and 2-6-2T no. 4127 propels a car train into the dock on 14th July 1958. The busy signal box had 54 levers and was known as Station box. The 68-lever Junction box was ¼-mile to the east; both closed on 15th March 1971. The next picture was taken a few minutes later. (H.C.Casserley)

69.　　　The car train was composed of flat wagons and a coach, the door of which is open onto the dock. The centre wagon has a tarpaulin on its deck; your author (VM) hired one in 1959 for a charge of 5s, but found his Humber scratched afterwards. Mr Casserley was wiser and preferred to wash his Hillman Minx later. In the left background is Pilning Low Level and the approach road. (H.C.Casserley)

70.　　Experienced drivers reversed onto the train to minimise the delay to their onward journey. The four-wheeled Scorpion wagons are seen in 1960, not long before their demise. The nearest car is a Vauxhall 12, the 1946 model.　(HMRS)

71.　　No. 4129 has assisted 2-8-0 no. 2890 through the Severn Tunnel on 9th May 1964. The connections on the left from and to the down goods line were removed in 1971. The suffix "High Level" was in use from 9th July 1928 until 6th May 1968. (P.J.Garland/R.S.Carpenter)

72.   No. 47236 is returning empties to South Wales on 4th May 1983, while the tunnel emergency train stands at the dock. On the right is the down goods line which extends ½-mile beyond the station. The goods yard had closed on 29th November 1965. (T.Heavyside)

73.   The down goods line is out of view in this picture from 26th June 2003. Both it and the station were still in use, but the HST would not stop here. The service comprised an 09.33 to Bristol and a 15.35 to Cardiff, Mondays to Fridays. Prior to the opening of the Severn Bridge, many Bristolians parked here and caught a train to South Wales. (M.Turvey)

WEST OF PILNING

74.   Bound for South Wales, a "Castle" races down the gradient in about 1958. The crossover was in place from 1942 until 1968 and was controlled from a nearby ground frame. A footpath led to the lattice bridge, which no longer exists. (J.K.Morton/M.J.Stretton)

75.	The 97yd long Ableton Lane Tunnel precedes entry into the Severn Tunnel. A Swansea to Paddington HST has just left it on 16th May 1979. The two goods lines had been added in 1942. The second Severn Tunnel East box (26 levers) had been beyond this short tunnel from 1942 until 1969. (T.Heavyside)

76.	The short tunnel is in the distance of this photo of no. 158871 forming a Cardiff to Portsmouth Harbour service on 26th June 2003. The crossovers date from 1988-89, these allowing reversible running through the Severn Tunnel. Wessex Trains were still operating such units from Brighton, despite years of overcrowding and complaint. (M.Turvey)

SEVERN TUNNEL

77.   The crews of an up train gasp for clean air as they emerge from the sulphurous atmosphere, laden with steam. Entering at 25mph, freight trains took about 15 minutes to pass through the acrid bore and would leave at about 10mph. The assisting engine would be replaced by one at the rear of the train at Pilning, before entering the single line tunnel to Patchway. This was to reduce respiratory distress to locomen. No. 3167 is piloting in about 1949. (R.S.Carpenter)

78.   Other trains passed through in 5 to 7 minutes, but passengers closed all windows instinctively before entering in steam days. A view from the coach seen in picture 68 shows the tunnel atmosphere to be clearer, due to the ventilation system. It also reveals the means of securing the cars and also the tarpaulins. (H.C.Casserley)

79.   Two Cornish beam engines were housed at Sea Wall, Pilning, these operating massive pumps until electric ones were provided in 1961. These have a capacity of 80,000 gallons per hour. The shaft is used for ventilation. The two photographs are from 1960. (H.C.Casserley)

80.   The eastern portal was recorded on 16th May 1979 as a Paddington to Swansea HST roared into the gloom. A Sprinter from Portsmouth Harbour did so on 7th December 1991 and collided with a slow moving HST. The cause was never established; it was either driver error or a signalling fault. (T.Heavyside)

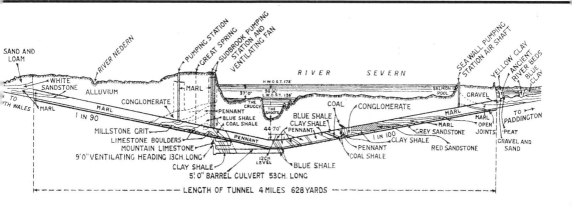

SAND AND LOAM — WHITE SANDSTONE — ALLUVIUM — CONGLOMERATE — MARL — 1 IN 90 — MILLSTONE GRIT — LIMESTONE BOULDERS — MOUNTAIN LIMESTONE — 9'0" VENTILATING HEADING 13CH. LONG — CLAY SHALE — 5' 0" BARREL CULVERT 53CH. LONG — RIVER NEDERN — PUMPING STATION — GREAT SPRING — SUDBROOK PUMPING STATION AND VENTILATING FAN — MARL — THE CRUGGY — THE SHOOTS — PENNANT — BLUE SHALE — COAL SHALE — 44·70' — PENNANT — RIVER SEVERN — H.W.O.S.T. 178' — 37'0" — 98·30 L.W.O.S.T. 156' — BLUE SHALE — CLAY SHALE — PENNANT — 12CH LEVEL — BLUE SHALE — COAL SHALE — PENNANT — COAL SHALE — 1 IN 100 — CLAY SHALE — CONGLOMERATE — SALMON POOL — GRAVEL — MARL — GREY SANDSTONE — RED SANDSTONE — SEA WALL PUMPING STATION AIR SHAFT — YELLOW CLAY — ANCIENT RIVER BEDS — BLUE CLAY — MARL — OPEN JOINTS — PEAT — GRAVEL AND SAND — TO PADDINGTON — TO 'TH WALES — MARL — LENGTH OF TUNNEL 4 MILES 628 YARDS

XXII. The longitudinal section reveals the irregular profile of the bed of the River Severn and the location of the main shafts. The first flooding of the workings took place in October 1879 when a spring was encountered. The tunnel was redesigned to run at a greater depth, but salt water overwhelmed the project in 1881. Worse was to come in October 1883 when the Great Spring broke in, Sudbrook Pumps failed and a tidal wave caused mayhem on the surface. The minimum ground thickness above the tunnel is shown as 45ft. The redesign took the tunnel 15 feet lower, but increased the western gradient from 1 in 100 to 1 in 90. (Railway Magazine)

81. Inspection trains pass through regularly and diesel haulage for them was introduced in 1947, two trains often running in parallel. Patchwork was recorded in 1961; leakage is continuous in some parts of the tunnel, but other sections are dry. A culvert runs under most of the track. In 1929-31, grouting was carried out, this involving drilling holes in the brickwork and pumping over 11,000 tons of liquid cement through them to fill the voids, a pressure of 25psi being used mainly. The wall thickness is 2ft 3ins to 3ft. (H.W.Walshaw)

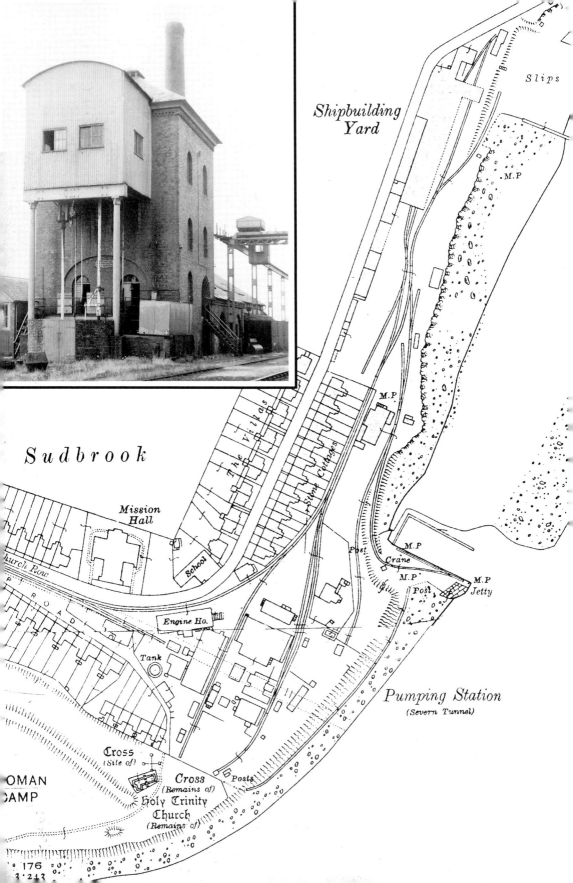

Shipbuilding
Yard

Slips

Sudbrook

Mission
Hall

Engine Ho.

Tank

Cross
(Site of)

Cross
(Remains of)

Holy Trinity
Church
(Remains of)

OMAN
CAMP

Posts

Pumping Station
(Severn Tunnel)

M.P

Crane

M.P

M.P
Jetty

Post

Post

176

(left) XXIII. The main pumps were installed at Sudbrook, on the north bank of the Severn. A branch from the Gloucester line at Caldicot was laid to serve the installation, mainly with coal. The 1921 survey shows that it also served a shipyard. For ventilation, a suction fan was installed, but this was changed to an induction fan in 1924. This was 18ft in diameter and rotated at 60rpm to force air into the tunnel, which required a permanent staff of 90 men in the 1930s.

(far left) 82. Three photographs from July 1959 follow. This shows one of the smaller buildings. It housed engines 11 and 12. There were seven plunger and five bucket type pumps, all provided by Harvey & Company of Hayle, Cornwall. There was a similar engine house known as "5 Miles 4 Chains", about ¼-mile west of Sudbrook. (R.M.Casserley)

83. Four of the beams in No. 1 Engine House are featured. The potential daily capacity at Sudbrook was 60m gallons, but the average quantity pumped was 20m. Serious leaks in 1924 and 1929 were cured by pouring concrete from above at low tide. (H.C.Casserley)

84. The largest engines had cylinders of 6ft 3ins diameter and 10ft stroke. During construction, there were 24 pumps at Sudbrook working in seven shafts. An amazing 36,794 tons of cement were consumed. Bricks came from Cattybrook, Fishponds and Staffordshire, the quantity being over 76.4m. Some were produced on site. (R.M.Casserley)

85. No. 1 Engine House contained 12 Lancashire boilers, each 7ft diameter and 28ft long and fed with coal by hand. No. 2 and No. 3 Houses coped with drainage from the bottom of the tunnel, while No. 1 dealt with the Great Spring. Much of the water was sold for commercial use. Today it is used by Welsh Water and Sudbrook Paper Mill. (GWR Magazine)

86.   The north elevation of No. 1 Engine House is seen in June 2003. It once resounded to the gentle rhythm of six Cornish beam engines, but the last fell silent on 6th November 1961. They were replaced by electric submersible pumps supplied by duplicate feeds and an emergency generator. (M.Turvey)

87.   The tunnel rescue train was photographed at Sudbrook on 26th June 2003, with no. 09015 on standby. Its permanent presence followed a critical report on the aftermath of the 1991 collision. A road/rail emergency vehicle has been available at the other end of the tunnel since February 1996. It is a 26-tonne 3-axle Renault and special decking has been placed in the track west of Pilning for transfer purposes. (M.Turvey)

WEST OF SEVERN TUNNEL

88.   The number of freight trains through the tunnel rose from 15,703 in 1897 to 23,122 in 1923, the pollution increasing accordingly. Thus a new ventilation system was provided in 1924. No. 5029 *Nunney Castle* heads a down train and runs near outcrops of White Sandstone. Built in 1923, the locomotive was preserved after withdrawal in 1963. (P.Q.Treloar coll.)

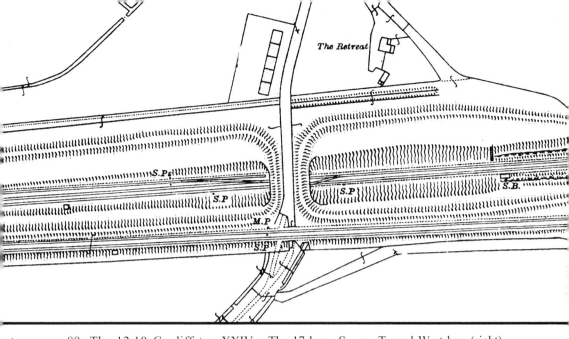

The Retreat

S.Ps
S.P
M.P
S.P
S.P
S.B.

←——— 89. The 12.10 Cardiff to Portsmouth Harbour was hauled by a class 33 on 27th April 1982 and was recorded on its approach to the tunnel. Behind the train are the steps once used by the staff of Severn Tunnel West signal box. (T.Heavyside)

XXIV. The 17-lever Severn Tunnel West box (right) was in use until 6th July 1969. The up goods loop is on the left. There was a second parallel loop between 1942 and 1969. The Gloucester lines are on an embankment across the bottom of the map; Caldicot Halt was built near the crossing of these lines and was opened in 1932.

90. Severn Tunnel Junction and the former engine sheds (now demolished) are in the background in this panorama from the bridge featured in the previous picture. Seen on the same day is no. 47083 waiting in the 1901 loop, as an HST accelerates down the 1 in 90 incline. (T.Heavyside)

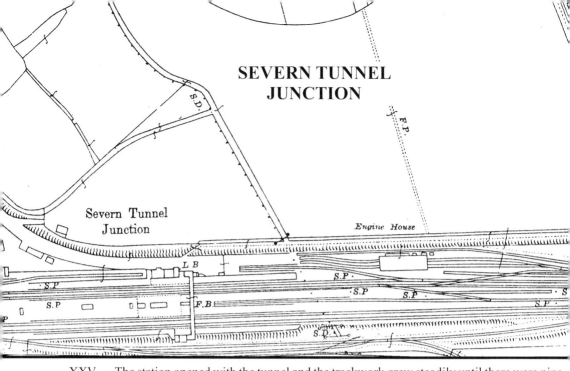

SEVERN TUNNEL JUNCTION

Severn Tunnel
Junction

Engine House

S.D.

F.P.

L B

S.P.

S.P.

S.P.

S.P.

S.P.

S.P.

S

F.B.

S.D.

XXV.   The station opened with the tunnel and the trackwork grew steadily until there were nine running lines parallel to the platforms. This applied in the period 1937-54. This survey is from 1918, when there were six. The carriage shed was incorrectly annotated as "Engine House". At the right border, the tunnel lines are above the 1850 Gloucester ones.

91.   A westward panorama between the wars includes one of the three bay platforms. Numbered 4, it was the only one designated for passenger trains. Standing between its two faces is no. 566, one of the Armstrong 517 class 0-4-2Ts. (LGRP/NRM)

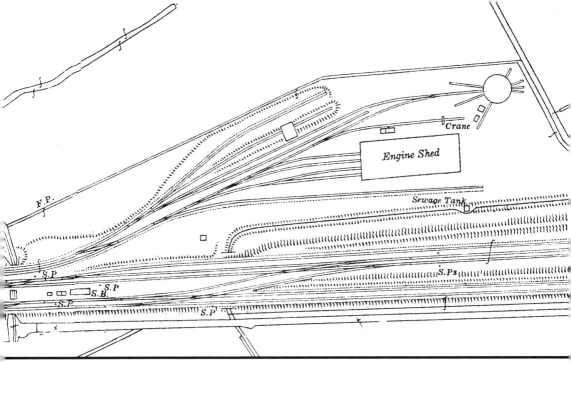

92.   The Pilning car trains used the dock at the east end of platform 1. Loading and shunting prolonged journey times, but there was a refreshment room at this end of the trip through the tunnel. The picture is from about 1938 and includes a Rover 14 (1934 model) and a Packard Super 8 of 1935. (Denty/G.Nichols coll.)

93.   Middle Box is in the background as no. 5099 *Compton Castle* approaches platform 1 on 28th August 1948. It was recorded as probably hauling the 8.15am Neyland to Paddington. The next photograph is from the same day. (H.C.Casserley)

94.   The main building is to the left of no. 6874 *Haughton Grange* as it runs into platform 2. The pens are to the left of the cattle wagons. (H.C.Casserley)

95.   The shed opened with the tunnel to provide assisting engines and also power for the numerous freight services radiating from the marshalling yards. The coal stage is on the left and nos 5253 and 6672 are in steam near the centre of this panorama from 14th July 1958. The right part of the shed had been added in 1931. The shed code was 86A. (R.M.Casserley)

96.   The other end of the coal stage was photographed on 12th October 1965, together with no. 7029 *Clun Castle* (now preserved) and 2-10-0 no. 92007. The shed closed that month and a diesel depot was established in June 1966, west of the station. The two sidings south of the shed were retained for unloading new cars. (T.Heavyside)

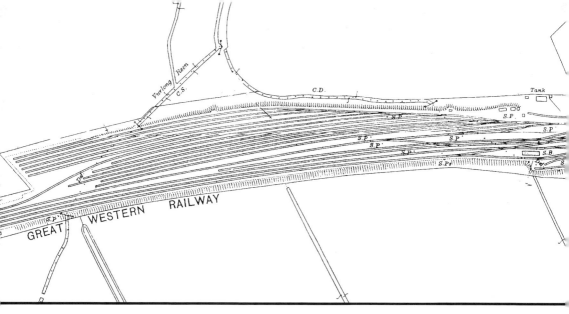

Vitelong Beam C.S. C.D. Tank

S.P. S.P.

S.P. S.P. S.P.

S.P. S.B.

S.P. S.P.

GREAT WESTERN RAILWAY

97.   East Box is in the distance as a DMU
runs into platform 2 in about 1965. Standing
under the massive water tank are the bogie
wagons of the Pilning car train, plus its two
coaches. (R.Holmes)

XXVI. This map continues from the left
of the previous one, the road bridge being
lost at the boundary. However, this section
is at 17ins to 1 mile in order to include the
full extent of the marshalling yards in 1918.
Upper left on the left page is "Bristol Yard".
This was extended westward in 1939 to form
an up hump marshalling yard, with three

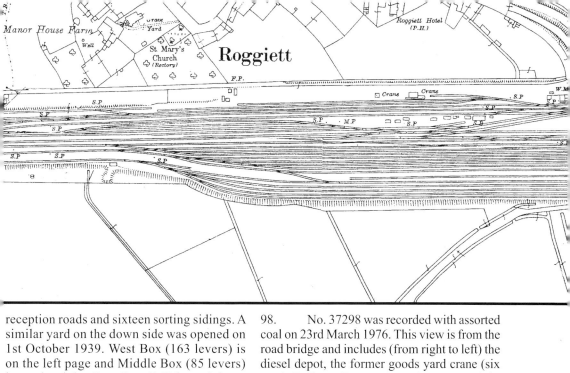

reception roads and sixteen sorting sidings. A similar yard on the down side was opened on 1st October 1939. West Box (163 levers) is on the left page and Middle Box (85 levers) is on the right. East Box (147 levers) is on the previous map; all three closed on 1st December 1968. The final numbers of levers are those noted.

98.   No. 37298 was recorded with assorted coal on 23rd March 1976. This view is from the road bridge and includes (from right to left) the diesel depot, the former goods yard crane (six tons), Railway Terrace (near the centre of the map) and the up marshalling yard, in the mist. Local freight service ended on 3rd May 1965. (T.Heavyside)

99.   Station staffing ceased on 6th October 1969 and demolition of the buildings followed, leaving this desolate scene to be recorded on 27th April 1982. No. 33030 is passing through with a Portsmouth Harbour to Cardiff train. The yards spanned a distance of 1½ miles. (T.Heavyside)

100.   Hump shunting ceased in both yards in 1981. This is the down yard in August 1982 shortly after the track had been lifted from the front of the hump cabin. Speedlink services were shunted on the level subsequently. At its optimum, this yard had seven reception sidings, the hump leading to 23 sorting sidings, behind the camera. Only three platforms (left) have been in use since 1968, the northern one being taken out of use, although still in situ in 2004. (J.Day)

101.   Two class 47s wait outside the diesel servicing shed on 5th September 1986, as no. 47249 works a Speedlink service to Gloucester. The yards and depot closed completely that year, with the loss of about 300 jobs. St. Mary's Church, Rogiet (new spelling), had just marked the centenary of the opening of the tunnel with the dedication of a plaque; the tower is in the background. (G.Gillham)

102.   From almost the same viewpoint, we witness no. 221103 *Christopher Columbus* running on a Virgin CrossCountry service on 26th June 2003. Introduced in 2002, the "Super Voyagers" (from no. 221101 onwards) were capable of tilting and also of speeds of 125mph. Much of the former siding area was subject to landscaping as a community project. (M.Turvey)

UNDY HALT

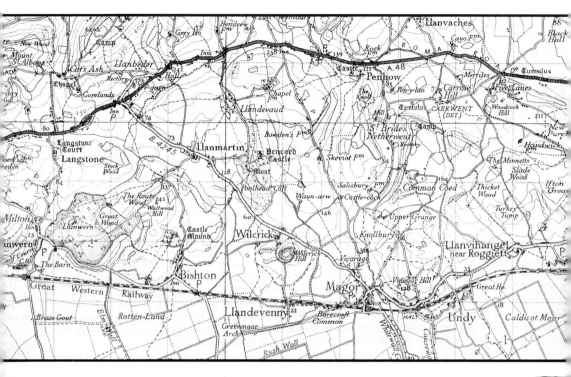

XXVII. The 1946 extract at 1ins to 1 mile includes three stations, as well as Undy Halt. This came into use on 11th September 1933. The reception lines and up hump headshunt came as far west as Undy Crossing (near Great House), where there was a 47-lever signal box until 10th July 1960. Moving to locations west of Magor, the level crossing at Bishton had a signal box on the south side of the line from 1908 until 1941, when the nearby loops and sidings were joined to form goods lines. A new box was built on the north side and its 38-lever frame was in use until 1961. It has subsequently served as a crossing box. The level crossing at Barecroft Common was closed permanently on 14th September 1941. A flyover for the up relief line was opened near Bishton on 17th April 1961.

103.   An eastward view in July 1958 includes the goods lines, which were added behind the platforms in 1941. Closure to passengers here came on 2nd November 1964. The outer brick arches date from 1941; the same applied at Magor. (R.M.Casserley)

104.   No. 47146 passes the site of Undy Halt on 5th August 1982, hauling a parcels train bound for the Bristol line. (J.Day)

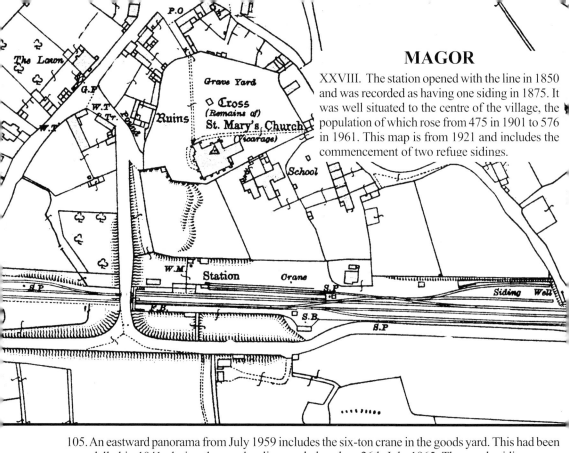

MAGOR

XXVIII. The station opened with the line in 1850 and was recorded as having one siding in 1875. It was well situated to the centre of the village, the population of which rose from 475 in 1901 to 576 in 1961. This map is from 1921 and includes the commencement of two refuge sidings.

105. An eastward panorama from July 1959 includes the six-ton crane in the goods yard. This had been remodelled in 1941, during the quadrupling, and closed on 26th July 1965. The goods sidings were used intensively to supply cement for the construction of Llanwern Steelworks. The signal box closed on 1st December 1968, having had a panel as well as levers since April 1961. (H.C.Casserley)

106.   Local passenger service was withdrawn on 2nd November 1964 and the platforms were eventually cleared away. One siding was still present on 16th April 1973 when no. 1710 (later 47121) was recorded with the 08.24 Manchester to Cardiff service. (G.Gillham)

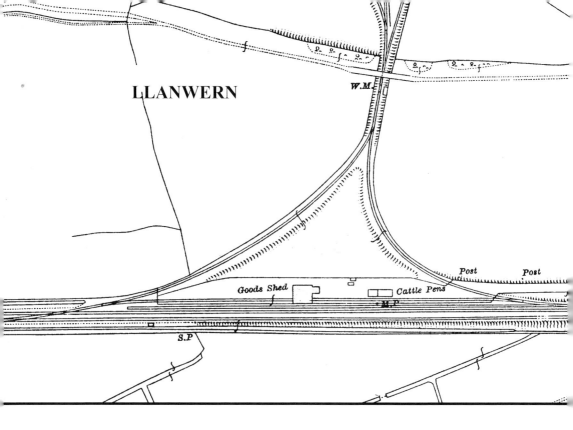

LLANWERN

XXIX. The 1921 survey includes the private sidings for lime, which were removed by 1927. There were 18 residents listed in 1901, the figure rising to 355 in 1961. All local traffic ceased here on 12th September 1960, as work was starting on the mighty Spencer Steelworks. The signal box (S.B.) had 40 levers and closed on 16th April 1961. The station opened with the line in 1850.

107.   Steel production started in the early 1960s and iron ore came in via Newport docks, coal was sourced locally and lime came from Buxton. Later developments meant iron ore and imported coal came via Port Talbot tidal harbour. Since steel making ceased here in 2001, slab is railed from Port Talbot and Lackenby, some being imported via Newport and Royal Portbury Docks. The rolling mills produce sheet for the motor industry and for white electrical goods. The owners have been Richard, Thomas & Baldwin, British Steel Corporation and Corus; they have shown a reluctance to allow photographs to be published and site entry is strictly limited. Seen in June 1987 are two class 45 diesels returning empty iron ore wagons from the works to Port Talbot. (J.Morgan)

Monkspill Cottage

F.P.

F.B.

F.B.

F.P.

Llanwern Station

F.B.

S.P

S.P

S.P

S.P

F.B.

S.P

F.B.

F.B.

108. The quadrupling between Newport and Severn Tunnel Junction was a matter of great urgency in 1941, as coal export from South Wales almost stopped due to the dangers at sea. The fuel was diverted to England, causing great congestion on this section of the GWR. This eastward view from near the level crossing on 29th July 1941 shows abutments ready for a new bridge over the culvert to take the up relief line. (GWR)

EAST OF NEWPORT

109. The 1894 Lliswerry Crossing box (left) is seen in July 1941, shortly prior to its demolition to make way for the new relief goods line. It would link with the loop in the background. The new box was behind the camera and had 41 levers; it was in use until 17th April 1961. The relief lines were outside the main lines until April 1961, when they became the southern pair. (GWR)

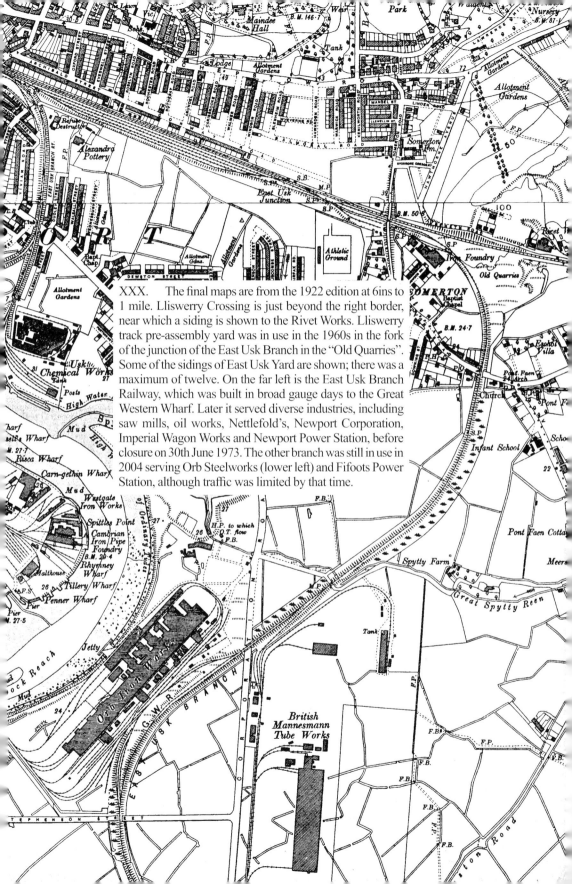

XXX.   The final maps are from the 1922 edition at 6ins to 1 mile. Lliswerry Crossing is just beyond the right border, near which a siding is shown to the Rivet Works. Lliswerry track pre-assembly yard was in use in the 1960s in the fork of the junction of the East Usk Branch in the "Old Quarries". Some of the sidings of East Usk Yard are shown; there was a maximum of twelve. On the far left is the East Usk Branch Railway, which was built in broad gauge days to the Great Western Wharf. Later it served diverse industries, including saw mills, oil works, Nettlefold's, Newport Corporation, Imperial Wagon Works and Newport Power Station, before closure on 30th June 1973. The other branch was still in use in 2004 serving Orb Steelworks (lower left) and Fifoots Power Station, although traffic was limited by that time.

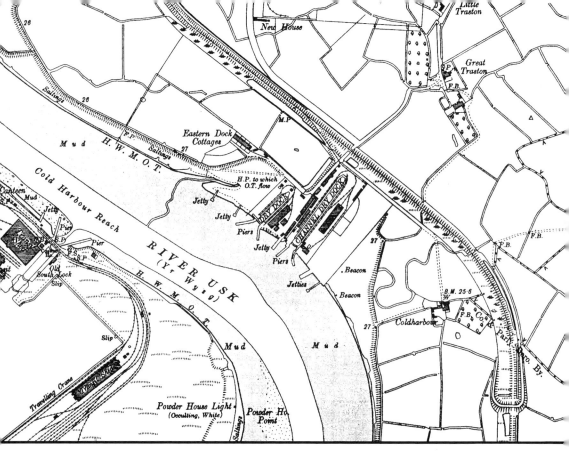

XXXI. This map continues from the bottom of the previous one and includes the siding to Channel Dry Dock which carried traffic between 1905 and 1970. The other dry dock had a siding from about 1920 to 1954. The branch was doubled in 1952 and the Monsanto chemical works had numerous sidings on the right from 1947 until about 1980. The British Aluminium Company had a network of lines nearer the river from 1938 to 1974. The track was doubled and extended to the massive Uskmouth Power Stations, where the branch ends. The first generating station opened in October 1953 and six coal trains were soon running daily. This increased greatly with the advent of the second station, almost ten years later.

(lower left) 110. Llanwern Steelworks is in the background as preserved no. 3440 *City of Truro* passes Uskmouth Branch Junction with a special train from Swindon on 20th October 1985. The branch had been singled by that time. The semaphore signal was still in use in 2004, although converted to upper quadrant. (D.Trevor Rowe)

111.   No. 37905 *Vulcan Enterprise* is eastbound on 17th August 1995 and is seen from the bridge on the right of map XXX. The oil train is the 13.25 Llandarcy to Llanwern. East Usk box (left) opened with a 39-lever frame on 16th April 1961. It replaced the 1941 70-lever East Usk Junction box, which was north of the track. (G.Gillham)

112.   Newport East box was at the west end of the Usk Bridge or Viaduct, which is 215yds long. The box had 96 levers and was superseded by a panel located almost opposite on 10th December 1962. From 1927 to 1962, Newport was the only major installation to have a mechanical route setting signalling system, the forerunner of which was installed at Winchester in 1922. (P.J.Garland/R.S.Carpenter)

113.　　No. D1007 *Western Talisman* hauls the 12.00 Paddington to Swansea over the River Usk on 5th October 1972. The locomotive was damaged beyond repair in a derailment at Ealing in 1973. The dock siding on the right was removed in April 1975. (G.Gillham)

114.　　The viaduct was widened at great expense by 1924 to take four tracks. A Cardiff to London HST has just left the station on 3rd July 1977. The first bridge was of timber and one span was damaged by fire before it opened. It was replaced with wrought iron, as were the others in 1886. They lasted until 1924. (T.Heavyside)

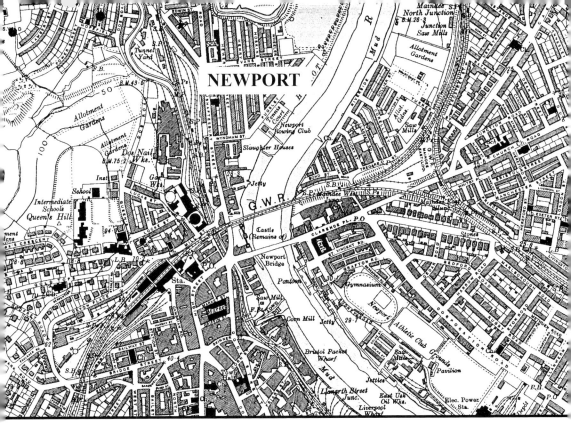

XXXII. This extract from the 1922 survey continues from the top left of map XXX. Top right is the line to Hereford and bottom right is the end of Nettlefold's line. The East and North signal boxes of Maindee Junction closed in 1961-62 and the sidings within the triangle have latterly been used by the engineers. West Box closed in 1927. High Street station is to the left of the river and is our destination. Running north-south is the line from Mill Street to Dock Street, which closed as a through route beyond Mill Street in 1963 and entirely in 1966.

115.   A photograph from about 1908 features "Saint" class no. 186 *Robin Hood* running as an "Atlantic". The first station had only two through platforms, but the 1880 one, seen here, had three, plus a bay and two through lines. The two earlier termini, at Mill Street and Dock Street, were closed in 1880. (G.M.Perkins/R.S.Carpenter)

116. The track was extensively relaid in 1926-28 and an additional through platform was provided on the north side. This was numbered 8; No. 4 is on the right and No. 2 is on the left in this 1930s westward view. In the distance are carriage sidings and workshops. (Stations UK)

117. Seen from the east end of platform 4 on 6th July 1947 is no. 5049 *Earl of Plymouth* with a Cardiff to Paddington train. The leading coaches are on the convergence of the through and platform lines. (H.C.Casserley)

118. On the down through line on 12th July 1956 is 2-6-2T no. 3170 with mixed freight. At about this time there were around 750,000 passengers booking annually and 300,000 platform tickets were issued. (H.C.Casserley)

119.   No. 50050 *Fearless* waits at the signal with the 06.45 empty van train from Milford Haven to Old Oak Common on 11th April 1988, while no. 37293 runs into the stabling sidings at Godfrey Road. These were subsequently allocated to EWS locomotives. (G.Gillham)

120.   The platforms were renumbered 1, 2 and 3 in 1961, No. 1 being on the right of this photograph of no. 66174, taken on 30th May 2001. It has had only limited use since 1961. The station was a busy place to watch trains in 2004; there were about 220 passenger and 80 freight movements every 24 hours. (M.Turvey)

Other views of this station in steam days can be found in our *Brecon to Newport* album.

Middleton Press

Easebourne Lane, Midhurst, W Sussex. GU29 9AZ Tel: 01730 813169 Fax: 01730 812601
Email: sales@middletonpress.co.uk   www.middletonpress.co.uk
If books are not available from your local transport stockist, order direct post free UK.

BRANCH LINES
Branch Line to Allhallows
Branch Line to Alton
Branch Lines around Ascot
Branch Line to Ashburton
Branch Lines around Bodmin
Branch Line to Bude
Branch Lines around Canterbury
Branch Lines around Chard & Yeovil
Branch Line to Cheddar
Branch Lines around Cromer
Branch Line to the Derwent Valley
Branch Lines to East Grinstead
Branch Lines of East London
Branch Lines to Effingham Junction
Branch Lines to Falmouth, Helston & St. Ives
Branch Line to Fairford
Branch Lines to Felixstow & Aldeburgh
Branch Lines around Gosport
Branch Line to Hayling
Branch Lines to Henley, Windsor & Marlow
Branch Line to Hawkhurst
Branch Line to Horsham
Branch Lines around Huntingdon
Branch Line to Ilfracombe
Branch Line to Kingsbridge
Branch Line to Kingswear
Branch Line to Lambourn
Branch Lines to Launceston & Princetown
Branch Lines to Longmoor
Branch Line to Looe
Branch Line to Lyme Regis
Branch Line to Lynton
Branch Lines around March
Branch Lines around Midhurst
Branch Line to Minehead
Branch Line to Moretonhampstead
Branch Lines to Newport (IOW)
Branch Lines to Newquay
Branch Lines around North Woolwich
Branch Line to Padstow
Branch Lines to Princes Risborough
Branch Lines to Seaton and Sidmouth
Branch Lines around Sheerness
Branch Line to Shrewsbury
Branch Line to Tenterden
Branch Lines around Tiverton
Branch Lines to Torrington
Branch Lines to Tunbridge Wells
Branch Line to Upwell
Branch Line to Wantage (The Wantage Tramway)
Branch Lines of West London
Branch Lines of West Wiltshire
Branch Lines around Weymouth
Branch Lines around Wimborne
Branch Lines around Wisbech

NARROW GAUGE
Austrian Narrow Gauge
Branch Line to Lynton
Branch Lines around Portmadoc 1923-46
Branch Lines around Porthmadog 1954-94
Branch Line to Southwold
Douglas to Port Erin
Douglas to Peel
Kent Narrow Gauge
Northern France Narrow Gauge
Romneyrail
Sierra Leone Narrow Gauge
Southern France Narrow Gauge
Sussex Narrow Gauge
Surrey Narrow Gauge

Swiss Narrow Gauge
Two-Foot Gauge Survivors
Vivarais Narrow Gauge

SOUTH COAST RAILWAYS
Ashford to Dover
Bournemouth to Weymouth
Brighton to Worthing
Dover to Ramsgate
Eastbourne to Hastings
Hastings to Ashford
Portsmouth to Southampton
Ryde to Ventnor
Southampton to Bournemouth

SOUTHERN MAIN LINES
Basingstoke to Salisbury
Crawley to Littlehampton
Dartford to Sittingbourne
East Croydon to Three Bridges
Epsom to Horsham
Exeter to Barnstaple
Exeter to Tavistock
London Bridge to East Croydon
Orpington to Tonbridge
Tonbridge to Hastings
Salisbury to Yeovil
Sittingbourne to Ramsgate
Swanley to Ashford
Tavistock to Plymouth
Three Bridges to Brighton
Victoria to Bromley South
Victoria to East Croydon
Waterloo to Windsor
Waterloo to Woking
Woking to Portsmouth
Woking to Southampton
Yeovil to Exeter

EASTERN MAIN LINES
Barking to Southend
Ely to Kings Lynn
Ely to Norwich
Fenchurch Street to Barking
Hitchin to Peterborough
Ilford to Shenfield
Ipswich to Saxmundham
Liverpool Street to Ilford
Saxmundham to Yarmouth
Tilbury Loop

WESTERN MAIN LINES
Banbury to Birmingham
Bristol to Taunton
Didcot to Banbury
Didcot to Swindon
Ealing to Slough
Exeter to Newton Abbot
Moreton-in-Marsh to Worcester
Newton Abbot to Plymouth
Newbury to Westbury
Oxford to Moreton-in-Marsh
Paddington to Ealing
Paddington to Princes Risborough
Plymouth to St. Austell
Princes Risborough to Banbury
Reading to Didcot
Slough to Newbury
St. Austell to Penzance
Swindon to Bristol
Swindon to Newport
Taunton to Exeter
Westbury to Taunton

MIDLAND MAIN LINES
St. Albans to Bedford
Euston to Harrow & Wealdstone
Gloucester to Bristol
Harrow to Watford
St. Pancras to St. Albans

COUNTRY RAILWAY ROUTES
Abergavenny to Merthyr
Andover to Southampton
Bath to Evercreech Junction
Bath Green Park to Bristol
Bournemouth to Evercreech Junction
Brecon to Newport
Burnham to Evercreech Junction
Cheltenham to Andover
Croydon to East Grinstead
Didcot to Winchester
East Kent Light Railway
Frome to Bristol
Guildford to Redhill
Reading to Basingstoke
Reading to Guildford
Redhill to Ashford
Salisbury to Westbury
Stratford upon Avon to Cheltenham
Strood to Paddock Wood
Taunton to Barnstaple
Wenford Bridge to Fowey
Westbury to Bath
Woking to Alton
Yeovil to Dorchester

GREAT RAILWAY ERAS
Ashford from Steam to Eurostar
Clapham Junction 50 years of change
Festiniog in the Fifties
Festiniog in the Sixties
Festiniog 50 years of enterprise
Isle of Wight Lines 50 years of change
Railways to Victory 1944-46
Return to Blaenau 1970-82
SECR Centenary album
Talyllyn 50 years of change
Wareham to Swanage 50 years of change
Yeovil 50 years of change

LONDON SUBURBAN RAILWAYS
Caterham and Tattenham Corner
Charing Cross to Dartford
Clapham Jn. to Beckenham Jn.
Crystal Palace (HL) & Catford Loop
East London Line
Finsbury Park to Alexandra Palace
Holborn Viaduct to Lewisham
Kingston and Hounslow Loops
Lewisham to Dartford
Liverpool Street to Chingford
Mitcham Junction Lines
North London Line
South London Line
West Croydon to Epsom
West London Line
Willesden Junction to Richmond
Wimbledon to Beckenham
Wimbledon to Epsom

STEAMING THROUGH
Steaming through Cornwall
Steaming through the Isle of Wight
Steaming through Kent
Steaming through West Hants

TRAMWAY CLASSICS
Aldgate & Stepney Tramways
Barnet & Finchley Tramways
Bath Tramways
Brighton's Tramways
Bristol's Tramways
Burton & Ashby Tramways
Camberwell & W.Norwood Tramway
Clapham & Streatham Tramways
Croydon's Tramways
Dover's Tramways
East Ham & West Ham Tramways
Edgware and Willesden Tramways
Eltham & Woolwich Tramways
Embankment & Waterloo Tramways
Exeter & Taunton Tramways
Fulwell - Home to Trams, Trolleys and Bu
Great Yarmouth Tramways
Greenwich & Dartford Tramways
Hammersmith & Hounslow Tramwa
Hampstead & Highgate Tramways
Hastings Tramways
Holborn & Finsbury Tramways
Ilford & Barking Tramways
Kingston & Wimbledon Tramways
Lewisham & Catford Tramways
Liverpool Tramways 1. Eastern Rou
Liverpool Tramways 2. Southern Ro
Liverpool Tramways 3. Northern Rou
Maidstone & Chatham Tramways
Margate to Ramsgate
North Kent Tramways
Norwich Tramways
Reading Tramways
Shepherds Bush & Uxbridge Tramw
Southend-on-sea Tramways
South London Line Tramways 1903-
Southwark & Deptford Tramways
Stamford Hill Tramways
Twickenham & Kingston Tramways
Victoria & Lambeth Tramways
Waltham Cross & Edmonton Tramwa
Walthamstow & Leyton Tramways
Wandsworth & Battersea Tramways

TROLLEYBUS CLASSICS
Bradford Trolleybuses
Croydon Trolleybuses
Derby Trolleybuses
Hastings Trolleybuses
Huddersfield Trolleybuses
Hull Trolleybuses
Maidstone Trolleybuses
Portsmouth Trolleybuses
Reading Trolleybuses

WATERWAY & SHIPPING
Kent and East Sussex Waterways
London to Portsmouth Waterway
Sussex Shipping - Sail, Steam & M
West Sussex Waterways

MILITARY BOOKS
Battle over Portsmouth
Battle over Sussex 1940
Blitz over Sussex 1941-42
Bombers over Sussex 1943-45
Bognor at War
East Ridings Secret Resistance
Military Defence of West Sussex
Military Signals from the South Coa
Secret Sussex Resistance
Surrey Home Guard

OTHER RAILWAY BOOKS
Industrial Railways of the South-Ea
South Eastern & Chatham Railways
London Chatham & Dover Railway
London Termini - Past and Propose
War on the Line (SR 1939-45)